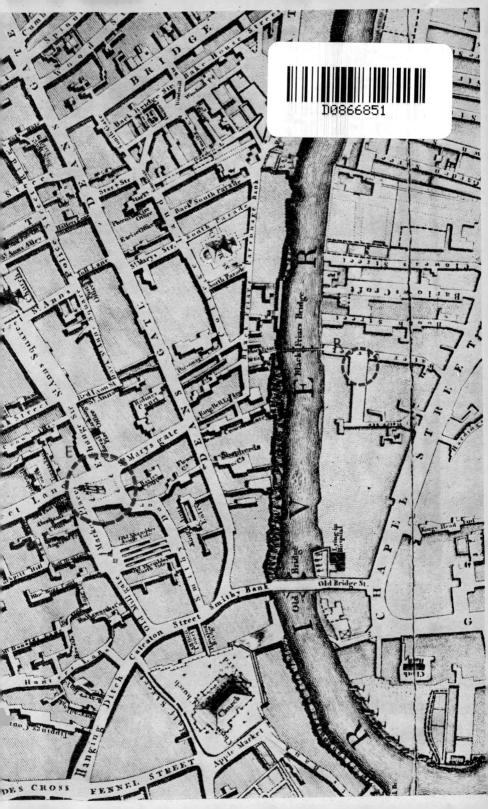

The
Early Manchester
Theatre

✠

The
Early Manchester
Theatre

BY

J. L. HODGKINSON and REX POGSON

LONDON
ANTHONY BLOND
FOR THE SOCIETY FOR THEATRE RESEARCH

First Published December, 1960
Printed and Bound in Great Britain
by John Sherratt and Son, Altrincham.
Plates engraved by the Northern Photo-Engraving Co.,
Manchester

❀ CONTENTS ❀

ACKNOWLEDGEMENT

The Society for Theatre Research gratefully acknowledges financial assistance from Granada TV Network, and from Mr. Neville Blond, towards the publication of this book.

✤ PLATES ✤

Preface

THIS PUBLICATION is the result of a long period of research, originating in a request by Mr. Sidney Horrocks, F.L.A., Manchester's Chief Assistant Librarian (Reference Libraries), for the co-operation of The Society for Theatre Research. Eighteen of the Manchester Library's excellent collection of eighteenth-century playbills could not be precisely identified: all were headed 'At the Theatre in Manchester', but they lacked any dates of performance or any indication of where the theatre was situated. These problems have been solved and the number of playbills of the same period has now been increased to thirty.

During the research members of the Society's local group discovered many facts about the beginning of Manchester's theatre history. Much information was obtained from an unpublished, undated manuscript by R. J. Broadbent, *Annals of the Manchester Stage,* which is available in the Manchester Reference Library. Other facts were obtained from newspapers, memoirs, local histories and periodicals. Although it is not claimed to be the complete story, this book presents the evidence obtained and attempts to give as reliable an account as possible of the two theatres that operated in Manchester during the period.

In the first section Mr. Hodgkinson deals with the building which was erected in 1753 and is consistently referred to by writers of the period as the 'Marsden Street Theatre'. In 1775 it ceased to be a theatre but the premises continued to be used for various purposes for nearly a hundred years. In an exhibition illustrating the history of the theatre in Manchester, held at the Central Library in 1952, it was possible to mark on a large map the exact position of every known Manchester theatre, excepting only the Marsden Street Theatre. At that time, with the aid of Broadbent, its position could be indicated, but only approximately. Neither playbills nor theatre advertisements in the local newspapers had revealed any mention of Marsden Street. A subsequent study of records of the town as it was in the mid-eighteenth century, and careful reference to original sources, has now revealed the missing information, which is presented here for the first time.

Mr. Pogson, in the second part, tells the story of the first Theatre Royal in Manchester, built only a hundred yards from the Marsden Street Theatre which it supplanted. It is significant that the plan of Manchester's first Theatre Royal is almost identical with that of the Georgian theatre in Richmond, Yorkshire, a building which has luckily evaded the juggernaut of 'progress', and is now restored as nearly as possible to its original form, unique as an example of theatre buildings of the period.

In connection with the preparation of this book a schedule was compiled of all performances advertised at the two theatres between 1750 and 1806, together with a card index of the plays presented showing when they were performed, and a selection of items of theatrical and allied interest that appeared in the *Manchester Mercury* during the period. Typescripts of these have been lodged in the Manchester Reference Library and in the library of The Society for Theatre Research in London, where they may be consulted. Each library also has photographs of the playbills. A history of one small corner of the English provincial theatre has been recorded.

PERCY CORRY,
Chairman, The Society for Theatre Research
(North West Group).

Manchester, August, 1960.

Foreword

THE NORTH WEST GROUP of The Society for Theatre Research was founded in 1949, and from the beginning envisaged that adventure in scholarship and detection which has found its conclusion, eleven years later, in the publication of this book, built not only on the work of its two authors but also on the labours of those many assistants who have delved among documents and maps and playbills and newspapers in quest of that elusive early Manchester Theatre. The Society for Theatre Research is grateful both to them and to the City Librarian and staff of the Reference Library, Manchester, where so much of the material necessary to the investigation is collected. All the illustrations have been provided by the Reference Library and are reproduced by kind permission of the Manchester Libraries Committee.

It will be useful to collect in one place a few notes upon these illustrations. Blackfriars Bridge is said to have been built by the players themselves to encourage their patrons to adventure across the river. The (?) 1743 bill is the earliest in the Manchester Reference Library, and the only complete bill for a performance at the Exchange. The picture of the Marsden Street Theatre is a drawing taken from a photograph of an earlier drawing which R. J. Broadbent had collected as an illustration for his book.

The ground plan is an enlargement from the Ordnance Survey of 1849, which is also reproduced in a larger section. It is a little confusing to find the old Theatre Royal there marked as 'The Queen's Theatre', but the explanation is simple. The building of the new Theatre Royal in 1807 did not involve the destruction of the old one, which continued as a theatre for sixty-two years, known first as the Minor Theatre, and after the accession of Queen

Victoria as the Queen's Theatre. With that last phase of its story this book is not concerned.

The handsome playbill announcing Mrs. Siddons for 'positively the last time of her performing this season' is a pleasant example of managerial practice. The bill for the following evening announces 'Mrs. Siddons's last night'.

On the endpapers, reproduced from a map of 1793, the Theatre Royal and the site of the Marsden Street Theatre (M) have been outlined in red. Circles round Market Place and the neighbourhood of Water Street indicate the approximate positions of the old Exchange (E) and the Riding School (R).

I am grateful to Mr. Basil Francis for collaborating in the preparation of the text for press, and in the reading of proofs. Finally, as well as to those who made this book, the Society's thanks are greatly due to Granada Television Network and to Mr. Neville Blond, whose generous contributions have helped to make its publication possible. From first to last *The Early Manchester Theatre* has indeed been a notable exercise in co-operation.

V. C. CLINTON-BADDELEY,
General Editor of Publications for
The Society for Theatre Research.

London, August, 1960.

THE FIRST MANCHESTER THEATRE
1750—1775
by J. L. Hodgkinson

I

THE BUILDING

MANCHESTER was not a large place in 1750, but it was very alive, growing rapidly, and had already shown signs of that sturdy independence which has become synonymous with its name. Some fifty years earlier that remarkable young English lady, Celia Fiennes, had visited Manchester from Rochdale when she was making her great tour of England on horseback, and she said then:

> Manchester looks exceedingly well at the entrance, very substantiall buildings, the houses are not very lofty but mostly of brick and stone . . . here is a very fine schoole for young Gentlewomen as good as any in London, and musick and danceing, and things are very plenty here this is a thriveing place.[1]

Most of the buildings were huddled around the cathedral and the Market Place, and there were really only two principal streets, Market Street and King Street, though Deansgate was just beginning. There was one bridge over the Irwell into Salford, and Piccadilly was then open fields with a claypit, 'The Daube Hole', for ducking witches and whores.

One of the earliest surveys of the population was made in 1757 when the number of inhabitants in Manchester and Salford was estimated to be just under 20,000. The next was

3

in 1773 and 1774 by John Whittaker[2] for the Royal Society, and he estimated the population to be about 27,000. These estimates are much lower than that made earlier by Defoe in his *Tour through the Whole Island of Great Britain*[3] in 1724. He estimated the population of Manchester as 50,000, but this was probably coloured by his emotions over the miserable conditions under which so many people lived and worked. It is likely that the truth lies somewhere between Whittaker's estimate and Defoe's, since Whittaker counted people living in existing houses; those in hovels, and the homeless poor, would not be included. What is of particular interest to us is the fact that in 1750 this comparatively large population was still officially 'a village'; there was no elected council, no representation in Parliament, and law and order were maintained by Justices of the Peace and two Constables elected annually.

The town had recently been very much in the news also. In 1745 Bonnie Prince Charlie had stayed in Mr. Dickenson's house off Market Street (hence Palace Square) during his ill-fated march to London, and for some days the town was a Royalist citadel. It is not surprising, therefore, that for the next few years there was regular quartering of troops in Manchester.

There are no definite records of theatrical performances in Manchester in Elizabethan or Jacobean times. The first reference traceable is in the title of that much-discussed play *Fair Em, or the Miller's Daughter of Manchester . . .*[4] which was at one time ascribed to Shakespeare. It was written about 1590 for Lord Strange's company of players, who must surely have performed it during their provincial tours; but no record has yet been discovered of any performance in Manchester.

There is also an isolated reference to theatrical history in Hollinworth's *Chronicle of Manchester, 1656*, in which he

4

says, 'It is reported and believed that John Bradford, preaching in Manchester in King Edward's days, tould the people, as it were by a prophetical spirit, that because they did not readily embrace the Word of God, the Masse should be saide againe in that Church, and the play of Robin Hood acted there, which accordingly came to passe in Queen Marie's reigne'.[5] Which of the Robin Hood plays was meant to be included in the warning is a puzzle. The great majority of these traditional folk plays were associated with merry-making on May Day and other public holidays. They were so popular in the sixteenth century that Archbishop Latimer, in one of the sermons he preached before this same Edward VI,[6] complained that, when he had intended to preach in a certain country town in April, 1549, he was told that he could not be heard for 'it is Robyn hoodes daye. The parishe are gone a brode to gather for Robyn hoode'. But E. K. Chambers, in *The Mediaeval Stage*, probably gives the clue when he says: 'Some of these plays were doubtless Miracles'[7]; it can only have been one from this non-secular section which Bradford prophesied would be performed after the Mass.

The seventeenth century is also a Dark Age for the historian of the theatre in Manchester; only two extracts from the city records in Bentley's *Jacobean and Caroline Stage* give a brief reminder of the poor strolling players who wandered from place to place in Puritan times when no theatres were allowed to open.

1635–36 February 18. Tho Maskall a player and 5 more to voyd the Town.

1636 July 3. To Jon Costine a player with 10 in his company to avide the Towne and not to playe these Dangeuse tymes.[8]

Why 'Dangeuse tymes'; was it civil war or plague?

It is not until the beginning of the eighteenth century that there appear any direct references to theatrical performances in the town. These took place in the first Manchester Exchange, which was built in 1729 in the Market Place on a site almost opposite to that of the present Royal Exchange. Its large upper room (in 1761 there was a ball there to celebrate the coronation of George III and Queen Charlotte 'at which were present near 700 Ladies and Gentlemen')[9] was used regularly for concerts and dances and, occasionally, by travelling companies of players from the Dublin and London theatres, who came for seldom more than a few days as part of their provincial summer tours. Broadbent tells us that Farquhar's *Recruiting Officer* was given there in 1743 and *Macbeth* and *Cato* in 1750.[10] The Central Library possesses a perfect copy of a playbill for a performance by a company under Mr. Heron's management of *The Recruiting Officer* 'At the Exchange', and an imperfect one, naming the same players, for a performance of *The Fair Penitent* eleven days later. Neither of the playbills is dated, but one has been marked '1743'.

It has been suggested by Joseph Aston, author of *The Manchester Guide,* 1804, that 'the earliest building to be used as a theatre in Manchester was not the Exchange but a temporary one of timber erected on the ground lately occupied as the Police Office at the bottom of King Street'; he gives no other justification for this statement than that it is 'recollected by the oldest inhabitant'. W. E. A. Axon repeats this statement in his *Annals of Manchester,* 1886, apparently ignoring the fact that Aston had meanwhile been severely criticised by that distinguished writer on Manchester history, R. W. Procter. In his *Memorials of Bygone Manchester*, 1880, Procter declares that Aston's statement 'accepted upon easy trust, has since been often repeated without sufficient examination but when put to the test not the slightest evidence is forthcoming in support of the hearsay'.[11] Broadbent, however, also refers to this temporary wooden structure and says that it was used by itinerant actors for a performance in 1735 of a play called *Anne Boleyn, or the Innocent Sacrifice,* and suggests that this was probably based on John Banks's tragedy *Virtue Betray'd or Anna Bullen,* but gives no indication of the source of his information.[12] Whether this earlier building ever existed and whether it was used by actors must therefore still remain in some doubt.

An enquiry into the origins of the first real theatre was the task which the Manchester group of The Society for Theatre Research had set itself. No contemporary account had been found of exactly where the theatre was erected, nor of its design; nor was the date known. The building is now always referred to as the Marsden Street Theatre, but none of the contemporary references to 'The Theatre' ever mentions Marsden Street. In the earlier years it is most often 'The New Theatre in the upper end of King Street', or 'The Theatre the top of King Street', and in later years more simply as 'The Theatre in Manchester'.[13] The King Street and Marsden Street references were puzzling and it was thought at one time that they might have been two different buildings. John Berry's map of Manchester, advertised in November, 1752, as 'Just come down from London'[14] shows Marsden Street as a very short street running west off Market Street into Marsden Square (still there), and what we now know as Marsden Street is a narrow lane which he calls Marsden Court. Even in 1772, when the first Manchester Directory was published by Mrs. Elizabeth Raffald, there is no mention of Marsden Street; but she refers to it in the second edition the following year, calling it 'Marsden's Street' and naming four manufacturers' premises in it. The street is also given in Whittaker's *Enumeration* for the same year (vol. i), and he lists six houses. But neither Mrs. Raffald nor Whittaker included maps with their publications,

7

and the exact position of the street to which they refer remained in doubt.

Mrs. Raffald, however, had given a tantalizing clue about the existence of the theatre; under letter 'B' there was this entry for 1773:

Baker, Thomas. Victualler, Rams Head. At the Theatre.

A further clue was found in Edmond Holme's much later *Directory of the Towns of Manchester and Salford,* published in 1788. This gives:

Douglas, William & Co. Dealers in Cotton Twist and Weft at the old Theatre, Brown Street.

This directed our enquiries into the modern Marsden Street area, for, as the street plan used as an end-paper for this book shows, Brown Street links the top of Marsden Street with nearby King Street, the distance between them being so slight (fifty yards) that a building which could be described in the eighteenth century as 'At the top of King Street', and in the nineteenth century 'In Marsden Street', might very well be in Brown Street. The definite clue we were looking for came from Procter: he says that 'our earliest theatre' was situated at the upper corner of Marsden Street on the ground now occupied by the new offices of George Spafford and Company.[15] The Manchester Directory of 1827/8 gave this Company at 32 Brown Street, a corner site where Brown Street meets the top of Marsden Street on its side nearest King Street, and where are now the offices of the Commercial Union Assurance Company. If this was where our theatre had been then all the clues to its position would fit; 'At the Upper End of King Street' would be less than thirty yards from its south side—'At the Old Theatre, Brown Street' would be quite possible and might be a clue to one of its entrances—'in Marsden Street, corner of Brown Street' would make Aston[16] correct too—and Broadbent's 'on the South Side of Marsden Street near Brown Street'[17] could not be said to be misleading.

It was a search among the title deeds of the Commercial Union Assurance Company which provided the proof in the shape of an Indenture dated March 5, 1793. This document is concerned with the lease of the land on which the Assurance Company's offices now stand, and after defining the site by its frontages to Marsden Street, Brown Street, a back street and an adjoining building, goes on to define the building, then standing on the site, as 'all that Edifice or a Building thereupon erected heretofore used as a Theatre or Playhouse and since converted into and now used as a Messuage or Dwelling house and Warehouse'. This was the proof positive; Procter was absolutely right and the others were not entirely wrong. The only disappointment lay in the fact that no plan of the site or of the building was attached with the document, nor has one yet been discovered. A further search, however, produced two more interesting documents, one of which confirmed that the description 'At the Upper End of King Street' was used in the 1760's because Marsden Street and Brown Street did not then exist. This second document is similar to the one just referred to, but is ten years earlier (October 1, 1783) and here the streets adjoining the site are described as 'a new Street now called Marsden Street' and 'another new Street now called Brown Street'. The third document, also concerned with this same plot of land and dated October 2, 1783, is described on its outer side as 'Conveyance of the Reversion of the old Playhouse Manchester'. These two documents make together what was then known as the 'Lease and Re-lease' of a piece of land, familiar legal twins of the time.

These documents give the boundaries and extent of the land on which the building 'heretofore used as a Theatre' was erected. This land had originally been part of 'a certain Field or Close in Manchester aforesaid called the Conduit Head Field'[18] and was approximately 21 yards deep (on the west) from Marsden Street, 30½ yards (on the north) along Marsden Street, 17 yards (on the east) along Brown Street and 31 yards deep (on the south) from Brown Street; in all, 587 square yards. We are not told how much of the land was occupied by the building or anything about its structure.

The only description of the building, contemporary with its use as a theatre, which has yet been found is in the brief impression given by Thomas Snagg (or Wilks) in his *Recollections*. He came to join the players at the opening of the 1764 season and says:

> Next morning I sallied forth and enquired for the Theatre Royal. This I soon reached, plain and unadorned, having been newly built. I found a few workmen, a stage carpenter and keeper of the wardrobe, but I could observe no appearance of the splendour I expected. Every matter and decoration seemed to be upon a very limited scale. An hour before the appointed time for the drawing up of the curtain I went to dress. Here was a new scene of wonder—the dresses laid out, the dressing boxes arranged and all the common apparatus for the night in convenient order. The manager had a room to himself, the first male performer likewise a separate room; the useful plebeians, of which I made one, a general apartment for habiting. The heroines and principal ladies had likewise an attiring room and the underlings their cockloft or upper story to display and adorn their charms.[19]

There is an interesting contemporary reference to the position of the theatre in relation to the rest of the town in the *Mercury* for January 19, 1762:

> At the Theatre, the Upper end of King Street, remarkable for its fine air and retired situation will be opened on Monday, January 25th, 1762, the subscription school of writing, etc.

This gives us a fine impression of peace in Conduit Head

Field away from the hurly-burly and smells of narrow crowded streets.

The next reference to the building occurs eight years after it had been abandoned as a playhouse, and is in J. Ogden's *Description of Manchester*, 1783, the same year as the Conveyance:

> The Old Theatre is now converted into a news-room and tavern, with a cotton warehouse below, the assembly room being continued yet above which is large and elegantly finished.

This would seem to imply that the theatre had been a three-storeyed building; and the reference to a tavern indicates that Mrs. Raffald's 'Ram's Head At the Theatre' was still going strong though the players had departed. Aston in his *Manchester Guide*, 1804, merely refers to the theatre having been 'neatly fitted up' by the players; but he helps us indirectly to get an impression of size by giving us the dimensions of its successor, the first Theatre Royal opened in 1775. This, he says, 'is a plain brick building, scarcely worthy of the populous and flourishing town to which it belongs. It is only 102 feet long and 48 feet broad, and on the appearance of a favourite performer is found most uncomfortably too small for the audience'.[20] It looks as though the first theatre must have occupied the whole of the corner site described above, for even then its whole interior could only be 91 feet long and 48 feet wide; and presumably the new Theatre Royal would be an improvement on this.

Proctor tells us what he knows about the building which was still standing as he wrote:

> When Thalia and Melpomene, Apollo and Terpsichore, departed, with all their devices, from Marsden Street, their temple was converted into a news room and tavern; somewhat later, it served as a warehouse for cotton; next, it became the

School of Arts; again it reverted to the cotton interest; and in the merchant service it is yet retained. The original entrance to the gallery, though long bricked up, is still distinctly traceable, part of the framework and one or two broken steps being allowed to remain.[21]

It is a pity he does not tell us where this gallery entrance was, nor indeed where the main entrance was. Could this have been in Brown Street, the address used by the occupier thirteen years after the players had gone, or was it really in Marsden Street as Aston, Proctor and Axon all suggest by naming the theatre after it?

Another and equally tantalizing reference to the building is made by Will Dinsmore, who also knew it before it was pulled down. After recalling Ogden's description in 1783 he comments:

I recollect the building and as a specimen of architecture it was a mean and poor sample. I believe about the year 1852 the classes connected with the Manchester School of Design met in the place for a short time.[22]

How regrettable that Dinsmore, who made sketches of a number of other old Manchester theatres, did not make one of this, the first. Or did he, and if so, where is it? He is confirmed in his belief, however: Adshead's Map of Manchester, 1850, clearly marks the site 'Government School of Design'.

Broadbent does not describe the old building, either, but tells something more about its post-theatre history:

Previous to its demolition, it was put to uses very different from its original one. At one time it was the home of the Manchester Law Library, and afterwards, it again became a theatre, but this time a gruesome theatre of Anatomy. Finally it was transformed into a Warehouse. During its occupancy by a firm of Merchants many years ago there still remained a time-honoured relic of the primeval playhouse, in the shape of an old fashioned glass chandelier fitted with sockets for holding wax candles, and suspended from one of the ceilings in the warehouse.[23]

According to him the building was pulled down in 1869, the same year in which its successor (then known as the Queen's Theatre) was also demolished.

There are some references contemporary with its use as a theatre however, which, though they do not actually describe it, give valuable hints about the amenities provided. The earliest one appears in the *Mercury* for November 13, 1753, and is the earliest indication we have found of the theatre's existence.

> For the benefit of Mr. Wainwright.
>
> At the New Theatre, the Upper End of King Street, in Manchester, on Friday the 16th of November 1753 will be performed A Grand Concert of Vocal and Instrumental Music, with Concertos on the harpsichord, perform'd by the best hands, and collected from the most eminent Master.
>
> After the concert will be a Ball for the Gentlemen and Ladies.

Clearly there was a room for dancing presumably the assembly room 'yet above', as Ogden describes it, and this sort of announcement is repeated many times in subsequent advertisements for both concerts and plays. One of these adds, somewhat plaintively, 'It is hoped the Ladies will come without Hoops',[24] and another, 'Followed by a Ball in the Upper Room'.[25]

On February 6, 1758, a performance of the masque *Acis and Galatea* was given in the theatre and is the first recorded "theatrical" performance there. The announcements in the *Mercury* (January 24 and 31) state that 'a large new Organ will be erected upon this occasion in the Theatre' and

> The Maske will be performed in the Lower Room and particular care taken that the seats are firmly supported.

From these and other similar announcements it is clear that the building possessed two main rooms, one above the other; that the lower was used for stage performances and the upper for dances and perhaps some concerts. If there was also a basement room, as Ogden suggests, it may have been used as storage and dressing rooms for the players. The tavern (The Ram's Head) could also have been below, though Ogden's description suggests that this was on the ground floor with the 'news room'.

There is one other most intriguing announcement in the *Mercury* at this time which may or may not refer to this theatre, but as it also brings us to the question of who built, or owned, or let the theatre something on this subject ought to be said first.

Nothing definite has come to light about this question so far; the only contemporary reference is in the entertaining but not altogether reliable *Memoirs* of Charles Lee Lewes. In telling the story of how Richard Elrington, a Dublin actor (son of Thomas Elrington)—one of the leaders of the Dublin theatre in the eighteenth century—and his wife, Betty Martin, brought their company to Manchester, he says:

> Their ill-stars led them to Manchester at the beginning of the year 1754. In this town Elrington took a new-erected theatre of a Mr. Magawly a famous short-hand writer.[26]

Lewes has the date and the spelling wrong, but there can be no doubt that he is referring to 'Mr Aulay Macaulay, tea-man, St. Ann's Square'[27] whose advertisements of tea, coffee, chocolate and of his book *Short Hand or Swift Writing* can be found regularly in the *Mercury*. Macaulay was thus one of the many who followed in the footsteps of that earlier Manchester pioneer, John Byrom, the inventor of a most popular system of shorthand writing. But at no time does Macaulay advertise that he is the owner or agent for the theatre, nor have we found his name connected with it in any other reference. The brief announcement of his death on March 19, 1788, makes no mention of this either, but refers to him simply as 'a very considerable dealer in tea'.[28]

This statement by Lewes is the acknowledged source for Procter's statement 'the agent of the new building, situated in Marsden Street aforesaid, being Mr. Auly [sic] Macaulay',[29] and apparently also for Broadbent's: 'The first attempt to dedicate a suitable permanent edifice to the service of the drama in Manchester was the *erection* of the Marsden Street Theatre, near Brown Street, in 1753 by Mr. Auly [sic] Macaulay of tea-and-shorthand celebrity'[30]— though Broadbent gives no source for this more definite statement that Macaulay 'erected' the Theatre. (It is interesting that he mis-spells Macaulay's first name exactly as Procter does; in all the trade advertisements of the time and in Mrs. Raffald's Directory it is spelt "Aulay").

This is all that has been discovered in the search for the original owner of the building, but the Constable's accounts for January 22, 1763, have this entry: 'Paid to Mr. Oliver for the Guard and Storerooms at the Theatre—£2 12s. 6d.', and Procter in his *Manchester in Holiday Dress* says that in 1758 a Mr. Horton was then in possession of it and goes on 'the building afterwards passed to Mr. Oliver, in whose hands it remained until it ceased to be a temple of amusement'. He gives no authority for these statements.

There is, however, the strange case of Patrick M'Quoid, and this is well worth examination. M'Quoid lived in Manchester; he is referred to several times in the Court Leet Records as being scavenger and bylawman for Manchester, and once in the Constables' account (January 1, 1746) he is paid £4 9s. od. 'for rent and coal for the guardhouse'. Later he became the owner, as we shall see, of certainly two places of entertainment in the town, and sometime late in 1753 or

January, 1754, he went bankrupt. Under the heading 'Days appointed for the Payment of Dividends' the *Mercury* for January 29, 1754, gives the following:

> February 19. Patrick M'Quoid, late of Manchester, in the County of Lancaster, Vintner and Chapman.

Three months later there appeared in the same journal for April 30, 1754, this announcement:

> The Assignees of the Estate and Effects of Patrick M'Quoid, of Manchester in the County of Lancaster, a Bankrupt, intend to meet on Thursday the 30th day of May next at two o'clock in the afternoon, at Mr. Budworth's the Bull's Head Inn, in Manchester, in order to make sale of the large New Building in Manchester, lately erected by the Bankrupt, to any person that shall be willing to become a purchaser. The building consists of two large rooms, one over the other, of twenty one yards and a half long and ten yards broad. The lowermost Room is aptly contrived as well for a Cock Pit as a Theatre, the uppermost Room for an assembly room, with suitable Drawing Rooms to each of the said large rooms, particularly two rooms with cock pens fixed in them, convenient for feeding cocks.
>
> Also at the same meeting will be offered to Sale a vacant piece of land lying westwards of and adjoining to the said building of 21 yards deep and 12 to the Front.
>
> All the premises are held under a lease made by the late Mr. Thomas Brown, pursuant to a Power given him by Act of Parliament for that purpose for 99 years absolute of which .... are yet unexpired.
>
> Further particulars may be had of the said Assignees viz: Mr. Job West, Mr. Thomas Hardman and Samuel Worthington, all of Manchester, at any Time before, or at the Time of Sale.

This is repeated in full in the issues of May 7, 14 and 21 following; it appears again four months later in exactly similar form on September 10, 17 and 24. The series is once more repeated five months later on February 4, 11, 18 and 25,

1755, and, finally, on June 3, 10, 17 and 24, 1755. All together these announcements were spread over a period of sixteen months. What happened at their final meeting on June 26 the assignees never disclose.

The similarities between the description of this building and the ideas we have been given of the theatre 'Top of King Street' by contemporary and other references are obvious. It is a new building and the impression given is that it has not yet been used. The occupation of M'Quoid (Vintner) fits nicely with the Ram's Head Tavern we know to have been associated with the building and 'the vacant piece of land' fits almost exactly on to the Theatre site, which on its *westerly* boundary was 21 yards 16 inches long. If we assume that the theatre building occupied the whole of the site set out in the Indenture, then this vacant land on its west would continue in line with the theatre's boundary and for 12 yards further down what is now Marsden Street.

The reference to 'the lease made by the late Mr. Thomas Brown pursuant to a Power given him by Act of Parliament' is even more intriguing. This Act is dated 1727 (1. George II) and enabled 'Thomas Browne, Gent' to grant building leases of his estate in the town of Manchester. In one of such leases, dated September 29, 1736, and made between Thomas Brown, William Shrigley and James Marsden, Brown, with the consent of Shrigley, demised to Mr. Marsden for 99 years land and buildings 'commonly called or known by the name of the Conduit Head Field'.[31] Now this is the same land on part of which the theatre stood; the Indenture of 1783 already referred to describes the site as 'that plot and parcel of Land as the same hath heretofore been measured and set out being formerly part of a certain Field or Close in Manchester aforesaid called the Conduit Head Field'.

Whether these two pieces of land (M'Quoid's and our theatre's) are one and the same we cannot absolutely decide, but there is certainly ground for thinking so. Unfortunately, M'Quoid's assignees never give in any of their announcements the unexpired period of their lease; if it was, as we suspect, the Marsden lease of 1736 it would still have eighty-one years to run in 1754, when they advertised the sale of the building.

It is impossible, even though these coincidences are slender, not to wonder whether M'Quoid's building may not be the theatre; but before we pursue this tempting theory any further we must review what is known of the theatre's early history and then come back to M'Quoid.

The first public announcement which revealed that a new theatre existed in Manchester appeared, as already quoted, in the *Mercury* for Tuesday, November 13, 1753. The next announcement appeared two weeks later on November 27:

> We are credibly informed that Mr. Elrington, from the Theatre in Dublin, will on Monday next open the Theatre at at Upper end of King Street with a play for the benefit of the Infirmary.

But it is curious that there is no further reference to this projected opening, nor to any other performance, nor to the theatre itself in any copy of the *Mercury* which we have examined between that December 3, 1753, and August 19, 1755, nearly two years later. A 'Grand Concert of Music' is then announced, and for the benefit of the same organist and composer, Mr. Wainwright, mentioned in November 1753.[32]

What happened to Richard Elrington and his players? Why did no one else use the building for performances of any kind for nearly two years? Indeed the mystery is even deeper, for the building was not used for performances of *plays* until *six* years after Elrington's abortive attempt, though it was used very occasionally for concerts, displays of curiosities and oddities, fireworks and the like. Otherwise it remained empty during these years for long periods, sometimes being used as a guardhouse by soldiers quartered in the town, as in 1757 when the Earl of Home's Regiment of Foot was sent in November after the Shudehill riots and caused this entry in the Constable's accounts for May 9, 1758: 'To Miss Houghton for Hulme's [sic] Baggage lying two months in the theatre . . . £1 11s. 6d.' There is a similar reference on December 24, 1762.

The only account of what happened to Elrington and his company is given in those *Memoirs* of Charles Lee Lewes already mentioned; he tells the story in lively detail, but how much of it is fact and how much the invention of this most accomplished raconteur it is hard to say. According to him Elrington came from Buxton to Manchester with his wife, Betty Martin, and his company in the beginning of the year 1754 (it was, in fact, December, 1753); he hired the brand new theatre from 'Mr. Magawlay', says Lewes, and obtained a license with difficulty 'from not the best-tempered magistrate'.[33] He and his wife then had what they thought was an excellent idea; they posted bills announcing that their play on the opening night would be given 'for the benefit of the Infirmary' (the first Manchester Infirmary had been opened in a house in Garden Street, Withy Grove, on July 12 the previous year) but, Lewes goes on, this brought upon them all the rage and indignation of the authorities, who were insulted by the implication that the town's new Infirmary needed the charity of 'rogues and vagabonds'. In spite of their pleadings they were ordered to leave the town within twenty-four hours and eventually sailed back to Ireland, whence they had come.[34] The Act of 1737 had been invoked in full on the first attempt to open the first theatre in Manchester.

It has been impossible to check this story or discover more

about the incident; no trace of a reference to it can be found in the Constable's accounts, or the early records of the Infirmary, or in Buxton; nor can we say for certain who the Justice might be who ordered the players to leave forthwith. Probably it was Samuel Birch Esq. of Ardwick who appears more than once in the *Mercury* as the Justice before whom malefactors were taken for summary treatment. He died in December, 1757, and the first recorded theatrical entertainment took place in the theatre less than two months afterwards.[35]

The story which Lewes tells is reported in brief by Procter[36] and quoted in full by Broadbent; neither of them questions its truth or bothers to check it. If we accept it in substance—and there is no reason to reject it entirely—we probably have the clue why the new theatre was not, as far as we know, used by actors for over six years after Elrington was turned away. The gentry in Manchester had been mightily offended and the story would soon be known among the itinerant players coming into Lancashire from London or Dublin; they would give Manchester a wide berth.

The poor man who had built the theatre would find his hopes dashed, too; and perhaps he, or his agent who had approved the idea of a performance for the Infirmary, now found the severe frown of a Justice upon him. Letting the theatre for any purpose at all would not be easy. Was this owner Patrick M'Quoid, another Irishman, and did he within the same month go bankrupt? Or was the agent Aulay Macaulay and did he feel it wise to lie low? His advertisements disappear from the *Mercury* for some months just at this time. Did either of them put the building up for sale in the *Mercury* on April 30, 1754? We do not know, but it is curious that the period during which M'Quoid's assignees were trying to sell his building is the period when not one hiring of the theatre is announced in the *Mercury*. Yet, within seven weeks of the final meeting of the assignees to sell M'Quoid's building, the theatre is in use again (though still not for plays) and continues to be used intermittently from then onwards. It would not be unreasonable to assume that while M'Quoid's affairs were in liquidation his building was not available for letting, that it was eventually sold on June 26, 1755, and then came into use again.[37]

The possibility must not be overlooked that M'Quoid's building was not used as a theatre at all but was put to the other use for which it was said to be 'aptly contrived'—as a cock pit. Cockfighting was the popular sport of the day for both gentry and people; players, as we shall find in Manchester's history, had to take second place to these events especially when, as quite frequently happened, the same building was used for both entertainments.

In the earliest issues of the *Mercury* in 1752 there are advertisements of cockfights at the Exchange in Manchester[38] and the Riding School in Salford,[39] both of which buildings were also used as playhouses. 'Cockpit Hill' is shown on the earliest maps of Manchester, and still survives, though only just, to remind us that there was once an even earlier centre in the town for this popular sport.

In February, 1753, ten months before any announcement about a 'New Theatre', the *Mercury* carried this advertisement:

To be fought at the New Pit
in Manchester
A Main of Cocks.[40]

This is the first mention of a 'New' pit, but there is no indication of where it was, or who owned it. From this date onwards there are no further announcements about cockfights at the Exchange; they are always 'At the New Pit'. Announcements continue to appear during the period when M'Quoid's building was being offered for sale and one of these says that Wednesday, May 15, 1754, 'being the last day of Cocking will be a Ball in the New Assembly Room'. This is the first reference to a 'New' Assembly Room. Did the new cock pit also have a room for dancing? It would seem so; in August, 1756, it was used for a concert and ball[41] and on the following November for an 'Auction of Notable Paintings' which was to take place 'At the Large Room over the Cock Pit'.[42]

Later references in the *Mercury* however give us information about the site and ownership of a new cock pit. During the Races on August 26, 1760, it is described for the first time as 'The Cock Pit, the Upper end of Deansgate', and on September 29, 1761, as 'Patrick M'Quoid's Pit in Deansgate'. This is obviously not the same as the 'New Theatre Top of King Street', and cannot refer to the building that M'Quoid's assignees were trying to sell in 1754–55 since a building in Deansgate could not be described as 'held under a lease made by the late Thomas Brown, etc.' That lease related to land in Conduit Head Field which the early maps mark clearly as being between King Street and Market Street. There were therefore at least two buildings owned by M'Quoid, one of which is obviously the cock pit in Deansgate, and the other, possibly, the 'Theatre Top of King Street' which was also used as a cock pit. There was a third building associated with M'Quoid. On October 14, 1760, the *Mercury* announced that

The Firm Stand, built by Sandiford and M'Quoid, on Kersall Moor, near Manchester

was to be sold.

M'Quoid, in fact, seems to have been one of the earliest

of Manchester's speculators in the real estate of the entertainment industry, and eventually he suffered disaster, as have many other later speculators in the real estate of entertainment business, and had to sell. His 'New Building' was up for sale, as we know, in 1754; his 'Firm Stand' at the Races was offered in 1760, and in 1762 comes this announcement in the *Mercury* (May 25, 1762):

TO BE SOLD

The Lease of the Cock Pit, situate at the Top of Deansgate, in Manchester, seventeen years of which are yet to come. The said Cock Pit has upwards of 200 Pens, two good feeding Rooms and Rooms for laying of Straw all in good order. Enquire at the above Place.

N.B. There is one of the best Bowling Greens at the same Place.

(The number of years which the lease still had to run further strengthens the argument that this was *not* the 'New Building' offered for sale in 1754; *that* lease, by 1762, would still have just over seventy years to go.)

The announcement is repeated in the following week, with the addition of 'a good accustom'd Public House', but in the next issue (June 8, 1762) this devastating counterblast came from one Robert Humphreys:

Whereas the Cock-Pit at the Top of Deansgate, Manchester, was last week advertised in this Paper to be Sold, and the Publick House and Bowling Green to be Set [sic]. This is therefore to give Notice That the said Advertiser has no Power, Right or Title of any kind or Nature whatsoever to Sell or Set the above mentioned Places, but that Robert Humphreys, Gardener, at the Top of Deansgate aforesaid is the sole Owner and Proprietor of all and every the above said Buildings and Premises. Whoever therefore are willing to concern themselves about the above mentioned Premises are desired in the first Place to apply to the said Robert Humphreys who will give them a Satisfactory Account of all and everything appertaining to the above Building and Premises.

It looks as though someone may have been trying to sell a mortgaged premises without telling the mortgagor. Was it M'Quoid again? If so, it is the last we have of him.

The theatre itself was also used for cockfighting at this time, and the players were made to give way to it. On February 17, 1761, they ruefully told their patrons:

> The Cocking Beginning this ninth of March the Company are reduced to an indispensable necessity of having the remaining Benefits on Tuesday the 17th, Thursday 19th, Monday 23rd, Tuesday 24th, Thursday 26th of this instant February and on Monday 2nd March.

and on February 24 the cockers announced the first battles of the spring season 'At the Theatre, in Manchester'. In March there were simultaneous announcements of cockfighting 'at the Theatre' and 'at the New Cock Pit, the Top of Deansgate'. But the theatre (and indeed Manchester) was soon to see the end of this sport; and the final reference of all to cocks and the theatre comes on April 30, 1765:

> TO BE SOLD
>
> At the Theatre, the Upper End of King Street, Manchester, a Quantity of fine New Cock Pens, suitable for any Family's Use. For further Particulars Enquire of Thomas Whiteley, in Chapel Walks, who will show and sell the same to any Person or Persons.

It may be that these are the very pens to which M'Quoid's assignees were referring when they offered for sale some eleven years before 'a New Building', in which 'the lowermost Room is aptly contrived as well for a Cock Pit as a Theatre' and where there were 'two rooms with cock pens fixed in them, convenient for feeding Cocks'.

II

THE PLAYERS

No RECORD of the first performance by a company of professional players at the theatre in Manchester has been found; we can only guess, from the solitary announcement in the *Mercury* of April 29, 1760, that the first season probably ended on May 2. This announcement said that on Wednesday evening, April 30, 1760, being 'the last night but one', would be performed a Concert of Music in Six Parts, and that between the parts of the concert would be presented *Theodosius or the Force of Love*. Since it was the custom in provincial theatres for performances to be given on Mondays, Wednesdays, and Fridays, we can assume that the last night was the following Friday, i.e. May 2.

Broadbent says that a stock company was introduced to the town in 1759 but admits that the precise date cannot be determined. Procter says that it was in December of that year that 'James Whitley brought his Company of Comedians and began the first Theatre Season upon the new boards'.[43] He may be right, or it may be that it was not until early 1760 that this took place, for the theatre was being used from December, 1759, to March, 1760, for a series of concerts and charity performances, as well as a performance of *Cato* in December by boys of the Manchester Grammar School.[44] It would not therefore have been easy to use it regularly as a public theatre at the same time.

But the fact remains that the players apparently made no announcement in the local newspaper of their intention to come to Manchester, nor did they advertise in its columns until the 'last night but one'. This was a benefit for two of the players, who no doubt were responsible for the advertisement. We know that performances were being given during the previous week of April 21, 1760, because of a duel which was fought (and ended fatally) between two gentlemen who quarrelled while attending a rehearsal[45]; but there is no other reference to the presence of players in the town at this time. May this caution have been deliberate? Were Whitley and his players anxious not to offend, as Elrington had done six years before, by the blowing of trumpets too much and too early? They were evidently more tactful with those jealous authorities and this time their propitiatory offering was not rejected, for immediately after the season ended the *Mercury* carried this very interesting announcement:

> May 13. Yesterday was paid into the hands of the Treasurer of the Infirmary by the Constables of this Town the sum of Fifty Pounds, being a present arising from a concert performed by Mr. Whitley and Company for the civilities they received from the Town and without any solicitation from the Board.

This cautious paragraph also gives the first evidence of the presence in Manchester of 'Mr. Whitley', the touring manager who was to be, as Aston says, 'approved dramatic caterer for the town for many years'.[46] According to Lee Lewes, who joined his company at Doncaster in this same year, his full name was James Augustus Whiteley; but Lewes spells the surname incorrectly and so unfortunately do many later commentators, John Bernard, Tate Wilkinson, R. J. Broadbent and Sybil Rosenfeld. It is always spelled "Whitley" in contemporary newspaper advertisements and other records. Whitley was manager of a considerable circuit of theatres in the Midlands, and in 1760 was at the height of his powers and his career; for the next twenty years he was to dominate the theatrical life of about twenty different towns scattered across the country in an area bounded by Leeds in the north to Worcester in the south. A fuller account of his life is long overdue; we have been able to include only a first sketch of it later in this story.

The first mention of him to the Manchester public which we have been able to trace comes some years before this, in 1752, when the *Mercury* reprinted for its readers 'An Epilogue of Thanks addressed to the Ladies and Gentlemen, spoke by Mrs. Stanford, in Mr. Whitley's Company of Comedians, at her Benefit at the Theatre in Stamford, in Lincolnshire, on April 21, 1752'.[47] This is more than a year earlier than that newspaper's first mention of the existence of a new theatre in Manchester. It is more than likely that Whitley knew in 1752 of the project for building a theatre in Manchester, or even that it was actually completed; that he planned to bring his company to it and caused the announcement to be inserted in the *Mercury*. He had friends in Manchester and players in his company, such as Mrs. Stanford, who had played at the old Exchange, as we shall see; they would advise him and probably act for him in this way. But Elrington forestalled him (or tried to) and spoiled the opportunity.

However all this may be, Whitley was certainly in Manchester eight years later, was clearly pleased with his reception and intended to return. Before he did so, two other companies appeared close by, one in Stockport and the other in Salford. They were both London companies on their usual summer tours, the Stockport one being unusually distinguished, with Mrs. Pritchard playing Lady Macduff in a company led by Mr. Giffard, the actor-manager who gave David Garrick his first chance, and his wife. This performance took place on Wednesday, June 4, 1760, 'at the Theatre in the Hill-gate'.[48] Whitley's friends may have told him about this for on June 10 he (or they) once more reminded the Manchester public about his existence and his company's excellence:

> We hear from Preston that Mr. Whitley's Company are to perform at Chester where they begin the first week in July; and as their performers are now esteemed the best anywhere out of London there is no doubt of their success in so polite a City.[49]

This is the eighteenth century theatrical version of "staking a claim".

The Salford performance brought competition even closer. On Wednesday, October 22, a company of players presented *The Beaux Stratagem,* and Fielding's *The Mock Doctor,* 'At the Riding School, in Salford', and the advertisement added that 'The Passage to the Riding School will be well lighted'.[50] That same evening the theatre in Manchester was being used for a repeat performance of 'the celebrated Masque of Comus with all the Music, Songs and necessary decorations' which had been first given on the previous Monday. We are not told who was responsible for this presentation, but *Comus* clearly kept the Salford company out of the more desirable Manchester theatre; the Riding School was difficult to reach on a dark October night in 1760 and very few can have relished the trip.

Whitley then returned; exactly when is not announced unless it was with the performance of Allan Ramsay's *The Gentle Shepherd*, which the *Mercury* of November 11, 1760, says 'Mr. Whitley's company will shortly perform . . . with the original music, songs and every necessary decoration'. No date is given. Then on Monday, November 26, he presented *The Merchant of Venice*, by desire of the Free Masons, and in the advertisement he printed a whole passage of Nicholas Rowe's commendation of the play, to reassure his Manchester public. There are no further advertisements until January, 1761, but performances must have been taking place in December, because Mr. Richard Walmsley lost his drab cloth cloak 'on Thursday Night the 11th instant after the play' and offers to return the one left in its place if his own is forthcoming.[51] Regular announcements begin on January 7, 1761, always as 'Concerts of Music' and continue until Friday, February 26. The full details of plays and players are listed in the typescript summarised in the Manchester Central Library, and it is interesting to find in Whitley's company two of the players who had been in the performance at the Riding School in October, Mr. Corry and Mrs. Pye. They may have been local residents, as were Mr. and Mrs. John Wheeler and their daughters, Fanny and Polly. The Wheelers played every season when Whitley was in Manchester and became regular members of his company; Charles Wheeler, the son, was the original proprietor of the *Manchester Chronicle*.[52]

Before the season ended and cocking began in the theatre[53] Whitley once more made his offering to the Infirmary. On January 8, 1761, the *Mercury* announced:

> Yesterday was paid into the hands of the Treasurer of the Infirmary the sum of Thirty One Pounds Sixteen Shillings and Sixpence by The Constables of Manchester, being a Present from Mr. Whitley towards erecting a handsome Clock for the Use of the Infirmary.

Whether the clock was a happy inspiration of Whitley's or a hint from friends we do not know, but the Infirmary board was still considering what to do about it three months later.

Before he left Manchester again Whitley expressed his customary profuse and polite thanks to the public for the 'repeated indulgences he had received'; it is a fulsome valediction, and culminates in this quatrain:

> As much for Candour as for Commerce crown'd
> Shall MANCHESTER to latest Time be found,
> Then let me not the Shafts of Malice bear
> Since Honour holds its Habitation here![54]

He did not return for another four years. It is not known why Whitley stayed away. Possibly the reference to malice in the quatrain has some special significance. But when his company eventually came back in the autumn of 1766 he began an undisturbed nine years' association with the Manchester theatre which lasted until it closed in 1775. For the time being, however, James Whitley gave way to rival managements.

There is one further item to be noted during this season. Signor Luca' Fabiano, who appears in 1760 as a member of Whitley's company, was a teacher of dancing; he either came with Whitley or arrived about the same time. In the previous year he had been at the Crow Street Theatre in Dublin, but had not made much impression there.[55] He remained in Manchester for the next few years and his announcements became a familiar feature in the *Mercury,* where he is variously referred to as Signor Fabiano, Signor Luca' and Signor Lucas. The most interesting thing about him for us is the fact that at the very beginning of Whitley's 1760 season Fabiano announces that he 'intends to open his School at the Theatre in Manchester, this present Tuesday, October 28th, 1760, to teach young Ladies and Gentlemen a Minuet or Hornpipe, in the most elegant and genteelest Taste, and will continue to teach every Tuesday, Thursday and Saturday'.[56] He did in fact open it on that day at 2 p.m.

in the afternoon.[57] He and Whitley must have come to an arrangement whereby Fabiano held his dancing school at the theatre on non-performance days. This use of the theatre as a school continued for some years, and was not limited to dancing classes; the 'subscription school of writing' already referred to became a regular activity in the building during the months when it was not used as a theatre, with evening as well as day classes.[58]

Immediately after the players had gone the cock fighting season began at both the theatre and the cock pit in Deansgate, and there is something ironic in the announcement that the first contest at the theatre would be between 'cocks belonging to the Rt. Hon. the Lord Strange and Sir Lincoln Cotton, Bart'. In days gone by 'My Lord Strange' had presented 'his Men'; now his descendant presented cocks.

The fighting season ended, and then came the announcement (June 2, 1761) that comedians from the Theatres Royal in London would soon act 'in the New Theatre, in Salford'. Whether this was the old riding school under a new name or not we cannot say; but the first advertisement is for *As You Like It* on June 17, 1761, and the last for *The Suspicious Husband* on August 26. The company played on Mondays, Wednesdays and Fridays, but advertised only the Wednesday performances. It was for this season, and to make their theatre more accessible, that the players are said to have built a wooden bridge over the Irwell on the site of the present Blackfriars Bridge.[59] The bridge certainly existed, but we have found no reliable contemporary evidence of the players having built it.

It is difficult to find an explanation as to why these players (the list of names we have is very incomplete) chose to ignore the Manchester theatre and go to all this trouble in Salford; there are no further newspaper references to performances in the Salford building after this 1761 season, though Bruton would have us think that other seasons did take place there:—

> There was a small theatre in Manchester as early as 1753, but as a rule—as an old saying has it—Manchester people went to Salford for their amusements. For horse racing they resorted to Kersal Moor; for the drama they frequented the Salford riding school.[60]

There is no evidence, however, that Salford ever became the theatrical centre which Bruton implies.

In January, 1762, comes the announcement that 'a subscription school of Writing, Accompts, Geography, English, English Grammar, etc., on a new Plan, calculated to answer most of the useful Purposes of a liberal Education' would be opened by A. Walker 'at the Theatre, the Upper End of King Street' on the 25th instant. The announcement tells us that the school would be held 'in a convenient Room till the large one there is finished', so alterations of some kind were obviously taking place to the building. (Signor Fabiano had meanwhile gone to 'Mr. Henry's Boarding School'.)[61]

Shortly afterwards, on February 16, the *Mercury* carried this most significant announcement:

> As the season for using the Cruel Diversion of throwing at Cocks is now approaching it has been recommended to all the Justices of the Peace in the Kingdom, to suppress so barbarous a Practice. And as it is certain that the Setters up of, and Throwers at, Cocks, etc. (whether Men or Boys) may, at this Time, be very useful in His Majesty's Service, either by Sea or Land. . . . Notice is hereby given, that the Justices of the Peace in this Town, will immediately appoint a Proper Number of special Constables to take up all such Persons as they shall find employing themselves in this Barbarous Custom in order that they may be properly disposed of in His Majesty's Service.

So cockfighting in Manchester was doomed; the series of

announcements in May and June (previously noted) indicated that the pit at the top of Deansgate was for sale, though there seemed to be some difference of opinion as to who had the right to sell.[62] One cockfight announcement for this pit appears during Race Week on August 10; after that is not mentioned again until April, 1764. There is no further reference to cockfighting at the theatre after February, 1762.

The coming of the next players to Manchester was announced in the *Mercury* on April 27, May 4, 11, 18, 25, 1762, as follows:

> Mr. Ross begs leave to acquaint the ladies and gentlemen of this town that he has selected a company consisting of the capital performers from the Theatres Royal of Covent Garden and Drury Lane and proposes opening the Theatre on the 2nd of June with The Provok'd Husband, or A Journey to London. The Scenes are new and painted by Mr. Lambert.
>
> N.B. The Company will perform every Monday, Wednesday and Friday.

Ross was one of Garrick's company at Drury Lane and the original George Barnwell there; he brought with him from London, among others, Havard, Shuter, O'Brien and Didier—the latter having been in the Salford Company in 1760. Mr. Lambert, the scene painter, was probably George Lambert, landscape painter, who was president of the Society of Artists and died in January, 1765. The players announced themselves as 'His Majesty's Servants from the Theatres Royal', and their season continued until the first week in September, performances being every Monday, Wednesday and Friday, except in Race Week (August 9) when they played every evening.

These were the first London actors, as far as we know, to appear on this Manchester stage and Ross does not seem to have thought it necessary to pay any humble addresses to the public, or hard cash to the Infirmary. But he continues the training in good theatre habits, which Whitley had begun, by insisting that no persons would be allowed behind the scenes and, further, that 'nothing under full price will be taken'.[63] London and provincial managers, Garrick more than anyone, had struggled for some years to clear the public from the stage, and to stop the pernicious custom of admitting those who came after the play (i.e. for the pantomime and farce) at half-price. But they had had small success so far; every attempt had been met with abuse and violence from audiences and even from the actors, who relied on filling the stage as well as the auditorium when their benefit night came along. From the very beginning these bad old customs were firmly discouraged in the Manchester theatre.

The repertoire of plays was conventional for the time, but the old stock tragedies and comedies were interspersed with an unusual number of Shakespeare's plays. Shakespeare was popular at this time, but when he was played it was with considerable alteration, addition and interpolation of processions, spectacle and the like. So when Ross staged *Romeo and Juliet* it was with 'the Masquerade scene and the Grand Funeral Procession of Juliet to the Monument of the Capulets with a solemn dirge'; *The Merry Wives of Windsor* was 'With the Humours of Sir John Falstaff'; and 'King Lear and his Three Daughters by special Desire of Lord Grosvenor' would be Cibber's version with the happy ending. There were new plays as well; Whitehead's *The School for Lovers* ('the last new Comedy') and the first performances in Manchester of Aaron Hill's *Merope,* Foote's *The Minor,* Murphy's *All in the Wrong*. It was the sort of programme in which, though there was no playing down, there were no undue risks.

Towards the end of the season Ross arranged for a spectacular titbit for his Manchester audiences. The Coronation of George III and Queen Charlotte in the previous September (1761) had naturally given the London theatres an opportunity of adding one more magnificent representation to their repertoire, and provincial audiences, not having seen the real thing, were likely to be even more excited by a staging of this gorgeous event. Ross announced that he had arranged for the 'Coronation Regalia from London' to be sent up and that he would present the spectacle for four nights only.[64] This enabled him to extend his season for a week longer than he had previously indicated,[65] but he warned the public that his company could not play after September 8 because they must set out for London on the tenth to be in time for the opening of the Theatre Royal on Saturday, September 18.

The general impression of this first season by actors from London is that Ross had been successful, and his return with a larger company the following year would seem to confirm this.

After he had gone back to London there was a pause in theatrical affairs, and then came a short season of variety and pantomime by 'Francisco and Rayner, from Sadlers Wells London and lately from Preston Guild'.[66] The advertisements indicate a four weeks' stay. Then on December 7 Signor Fabiano announced that he 'purposes having his Ball on Wednesday, the 22nd instant at the Theatre, the Upper End of King Street' and goes on: 'The Door for the Gallery will be opened at Two o'clock and the Pit Door at Three. The Ball will begin betwixt three and four. Pit 2s. Gallery 1s.' So now we know that the Theatre had two doors.

Just before Christmas the Constable's accounts[67] help us to complete the picture of a building which served many different purposes at this time:

December 24, 1762. Paid clearing rubbish from the Theatre to make room for the Baggage. 2s. od.

Earwaker says 'The baggage here referred to was that of the soldiers newly quartered in the town'. These were two troops of the Royal Forresters commanded by the Marquis of Granby.

The theatre has few references in the Press for the next six months; Mr. Walker continues to hold his school there, and there was a performance of *The Messiah* for the benefit of Mr. Wainwright, the local organist and music teacher. But it sprang to life in early June, 1763, when Ross returned again with a London company and presented a season of plays which lasted until the first week in September. Their arrival is announced hastily, and without details, in the *Mercury* for May 31 and says simply that a play and a farce will be given on Monday, June 6, with dancing by Signor Tassoni and Miss Twist. The next few performances are not announced at all, but the *Mercury* of June 14 tells us that Othello was acted 'on Friday last' with Ross as Othello and Mrs. Lee as Desdemona. Regular advertisements begin in this issue, but only for one performance on each occasion and no performers are named, except Signor Tassoni and Miss Twist, who appear in every one, until the benefits begin on July 27 and the full cast is given in each announcement.

The season began with the well-tried favourites, the "safe" plays like *The Beaux Stratagem, The Recruiting Officer, The Provok'd Husband*, and *George Barnwell*; but towards the middle of the season Ross again introduced plays which were new to Manchester audiences, like Buckingham's *The Rehearsal*, Lee's *Alexander the Great*, Rowe's *The Royal Convert*, Brooke's *The Female Officer* and Farquhar's *The Constant Couple*. Whether these were a success we do not know, but the season ended with the Race Week and the old favourites.

One of the principal actors in the company was subpoena'd to attend the Assizes in Lancaster during the season, but the reason is not disclosed; this was Lee, whose wife was playing leads with Ross. The visit to Lancaster cost Lee his benefit night and he ruefully decided to share his wife's.[68]

Once again, as soon as the season ended, Mr. Walker published his usual announcement and the theatre became a school, with occasional use as a port of call for people like Signor and Signora Gurrini, who came from 'Edinburgh, Newcastle, and York' to perform 'Italian Musical Burlettas' for Manchester audiences 'in the same manner as at the Theatre in the Haymarket, London'.[69] And, of course, there was the performance of *The Messiah* for Mr. Wainwright.

Two other items are worth noting in the 1763 season. The company went off for a day on Tuesday, August 23, to 'the new Theatre in Stockport' to give a performance of *A Bold Stroke for a Wife*.[70] From the advertisement it would seem as though one of the company (Mr. Burden) had associations with the town. It is probable, of course, that there were other one night stands of this kind during the season, but this is the only one so far traced.

Another is the printing in the *Mercury* (of February 15 and November 22) of the prologues to two new comedies from the London stage.[71] This custom was a feature of the *Mercury* from its beginning, and is an illustration of how the interest of Manchester audiences in theatrical affairs was kept alive. It was also, of course, a subtle way of advertising; for example, the prologue to Colman's *The Deuce is in Him* was printed, without comment, in the November 22 issue, and when the players returned in 1764 this play was duly presented as a new comedy 'never acted here'.

Ross did not return again to Manchester; his next endeavours in provincial management were in Edinburgh and his story can be found in Lee Lewes's *Memoirs*.[72] The next two seasons in Manchester were under the management of John Lee, who had been here with Ross on both occasions. A notice dated 'London April 9th, 1765' appeared in the *Mercury* on the two following weeks:

> Mr. Ross, having declined the Management of the Manchester Theatre, Mr. Lee begs leave to acquaint the Public that he has undertaken it, and that he purposes to exert such Diligence and Regularity in the Performances as will, he hopes, conduce to render them worthy their encouragement.

This was probably an agreed statement between the two actors, but why Ross 'declined' is never told. Lee was a leading member of Garrick's Company and according to Thomas Snagg (or Wilks):

> Was a very excellent actor and trod so near the heels of Garrick that Garrick was fearful he might "gall his Kibe", or without a quotation that he might affect his great reputation. To avoid a comparison he absolutely engaged Mr. Lee at a good salary for three years, for the purpose, and literally did lay him on the shelf.[73]

The new company's first advertisement appeared on May 25, 1764; it announced the names of the players and that the season would open with *The Provok'd Wife* and *Thomas and Sally*. The first night was on Monday, June 11, and the players remained until the end of the races on September 7.

None of the actors who had been here with Ross was in Lee's company, and of the actresses there was only Mrs. Lee. The scene-painter (Williams) and dancing master (Tassoni) were the same, but it is likely that these were local residents. Lee's company included Love, the actor from whom Boswell took lessons in speech and whom Thomas Snagg describes as 'the best Falstaff of his time and perhaps the pleasantest taken for "all in all" since the days of Quin. His real name was Dance'.[74] Others in the company were Keasberry, and Banister; Mrs. Love, Mrs. Stephens, and

Mrs. Cooper, and 'a young gentlewoman who never yet appeared upon any stage', who may have been a Mrs. Vernon, named later on in the season as playing juvenile leads and singing songs.

This 1764 season also saw the debut of Thomas Snagg as an actor, under the pseudonym of John Wilks. His *Recollections*, written in 1810 and published in 1951 by the Dropmore Press, contain most valuable information and are the only original source, so far discovered, of information about the first Manchester theatre while it was actually in existence.

The company was not such a strong one as Ross had brought, and the repertoire of plays for this season was more conventional; but there were one or two unfamiliar ones, including a new farce *The Mayor of Garratt* by Samuel Foote, which was played frequently in the following Manchester seasons partly, probably, because of nearby Garratt Hall. One of the announcements of a performance of *King Henry the Fourth* adds 'in which, by desire, will be introduced the Cushion Scene'—but we are not told who was responsible for this interpolation. The occasion was Love's benefit on August 10 and no doubt he played Falstaff, so highly commended by Snagg.

From the very beginning of the season and in all his early advertisements Lee made it clear that there would be no late starting and no 'dismissions'.

> Mr. Lee begs leave to assure the Public that the Plays shall begin punctually at the Time advertised; and that the Audience shall never be disappointed by a Dismission upon any account whatsoever.[75]

Whether this had been a fault in Ross's time we cannot say, but Lee's anxiety on this matter seems an attempt to meet criticism.

A new feature was also introduced to the public; Lee announced that the 'Books of the Entertainment' were to be had at J. Harrop's, and at the door of the theatre, at 3d. each.[76] This was obviously a nice business arrangement between the manager and the local printer, bookseller and stationer.

Snagg has left comments on this season which indicate that it was not a very rewarding one:

> . . . we cut an appearance to grace a Bartholomew Booth. The town soon found us out, as players phrase it. We were not endued with attraction, and the business was exceedingly bad, there being scarcely sufficient money taken to pay the salaries.

His own salary was a guinea a week instead of a share, with the usual benefit towards the end of the season.[77] He describes his own benefit night with a rueful charm:

> When my own night came . . . There arrived a whimsical and perhaps fortunate accident to save my credit and account for the empty benches. The Reverend Mr. John Wesley came unexpectedly to Manchester and preached in a square near the Playhouse in the open air. As he entertained his Congregation gratis I acted hardly to anyone but to those who had taken tickets before.[78]

After Lee had departed there was the usual pause, and then the usual variety season; this time Mr. Mathews performed 'Several Equilibres on the Wire' and the celebrated Madame Lewvisico went 'through her whole Performances',[78] (After a month in Manchester she went through them again in Warrington and Liverpool.) An item in the *Mercury* for October 23, however, indicates that the theatre ran the risk of becoming a less salubrious place of entertainment:

> At the same Sessions two Persons who should have fought on the 1st instant, at the Theatre here, for one Hundred Pounds, were obliged to find Sureties for their good Behaviour.

Lee came back again in June, 1765, with Keasberry, Watts and Wilks from his actors in the 1764 company and, apart from his wife, a complete new team of ladies. Among the latter was the beautiful Mrs. Baddeley, who had made her debut at Drury Lane the previous April and was on her first provincial campaign. In the next few years she became the rage of London; her portrait as Fanny in *The Clandestine Marriage* was painted by Zoffany at the King's command and she seemed at one time to have all rivals beaten; but recklessness and dissipation ruined her and she died in miserable circumstances in Edinburgh in 1786. Wilks (or Snagg) describes her when she was with him in Manchester:

Mrs. Badderley [sic] then was an exceedingly beautiful woman. She played the ladies in most comedies and operas, and I, from figure and youth, was often allotted to be her lover before the curtain, which brought an intimacy, with many a cup of tea and private walk with her, where I have been charmed with her melodious voice. T'was then she smiled with innocence nor did scandal dare to breathe upon her purity . . . I'll venture to say she was the best and most beautiful Ophelia I ever saw.[80]

The season opened on June 14 and closed as usual with the Races (September 20). After they had been playing for a month Lee introduced his titbit of the season, a new pantomime which was to have its first performance in Manchester and was no doubt expected to improve business. The following description appeared after the first night:

Last night was perform'd at Manchester Theatre a new Pantomime call'd The Royal Hunters, or The Execution of Harlequin, which was received with the highest Testimony of Approbation. The Characters were all play'd with great activity and humour, the Deceptions were happily executed, and the Scenery not only local and well adapted to the Place of Exhibition but the Grandest that has ever been seen in this Country.[81]

The Manchester Central Library has the playbill of the first night, an early record of Manchester's love of pantomimes and premières.

Otherwise the repertoire is very much "the mixture as before", with quite a fair proportion of plays new to the Manchester public: Steele's *The Funeral,* Cibber's *The Lady's Last Stake* and *The Refusal,* and (author unknown) *The City Wives' Confederacy*. It may be an early indication of Manchester's critical ability that the last three plays were never seen again, at least in this theatre. Or it could be only an indication of Manchester's customary caution. Snagg says:

> Until the time of the races the business was exceedingly bad and had very little difference to the preceding year.[82]

There is news about the building itself during this year. On April 30, as has been already quoted, a quantity of cockpens was offered for sale and on September 3, in the notice about the arrangements for the Races, is this footnote:

> Manchester Races. The Dinner will be on the Table at the Exchange at four, and the Assembly begin at Nine every evening in the New Room at the Theatre.

This new room had probably been created out of the space previously occupied by the cockpens, and the alterations may also have increased the auditorium because Mr. Saunders, who came in December to entertain with his 'Equilibres on the Wire',[83] sets out his admission prices in a new way:

Pit 1/6   First Gallery 1/-   Upper Gallery 6d.

He reminds us too, by his N.B. in the same announcement, how cold it must have been in these provincial theatres during the winter:

> Fires are kept in the Pit and Galleries in order to keep the House Warm.

Another variety programme was presented in February, 1766, by the 'Fam'd Prussians', a team of acrobats. They stayed until March 18.

There was no summer season in 1766; the London players did not return, and never did return, to this theatre. We cannot find any explanation of this beyond the poor business recorded by Thomas Snagg, and to attempt conclusions would not get us very far. Players were in the district, but none came to Manchester. In May the new theatre in Wigan was opened; in August Manchester was treated to three performances at the theatre of Stevens's "Lecture upon Heads" and one of Handel's *Acis and Galatea*. In September some players were giving *Richard III* and *The Clandestine Marriage* at the theatre in Rochdale. The latter play was only six months old but was already in rehearsal there—smart work by a provincial manager. Was it Whitley? Both plays were in his repertory for the forthcoming Manchester season.

It was in October, 1766, that James Whitley returned to the building which he had probably opened almost seven years before, and began the series of regular winter performances which lasted until May, 1775.

III

JAMES WHITLEY

THIS IS the moment to pause in our story and pay some attention to the man who brought his players to the town for eleven of the fifteen 'seasons' known to have taken place in the first Manchester theatre. Whitley was a most remarkable man and had more to do with the development of the provincial theatre in the eighteenth century than he has ever been given credit for. Even in this incomplete record we have traced him between 1750 and 1781 as a manager in nineteen different towns, in some of which he was responsible for actually building the first public theatre. In the memoirs of his contemporaries, as well as of those who came after him, he is always referred to with affection and respect even if with amused tolerance of his so-called eccentricities. He was undoubtedly most passionate in his devotion to the theatre, and he was a true "provincial"; he never ached for London and its glories but rather despised those who did. Perhaps he knew his own limitations better than some of his critics, and that his chances of success would never be found there. He lived the whole of his life in the company of the lesser known players whose story makes up the true beginnings of our provincial theatre, and within that range he was always an influence for good and frequently a pioneer.

The first part of his life is colourfully sketched in by Charles Lee Lewes who, as a young actor of twenty, first met Whitley in 1760; his memoirs are the only source of infor-

mation about Whitley's boyhood and beginnings in the
theatre.[84] He was born, says Lewes, in or near Dublin where
his father, a private in the St. George's Light Dragoons, was
stationed, and though Lewes omits the year it is probable
from later references that this was about 1724 or 1725. The
family was very poor and the father, a sick man, an out-
patient of Kilmainham Hospital. Young Whitley had no
schooling but was taught to read and write by a solicitor who
employed him as a messenger; later the solicitor was jailed
for debt but the boy continued to serve him, as well as
obtaining many jobs besides as a hack writer. All this sounds
a most unpromising beginning for a lad who was soon to
become a player and remain so for the rest of his life; but it
was in fact while he was attending on his employer in the
prison that Whitley met Joseph Elrington, an actor at the
Dublin theatre who was visiting a friend in the same prison.
Elrington took to the 'shrewd and sensible lad' and introduced him to the prompter at the Smock Alley Theatre
where the Elrington family was already famous.

The prompter at that time was William Rufus Chetwood
and it was he who gave Whitley his first job in a theatre.
The boy was engaged to write out parts at a penny a length
(42 lines) for Chetwood, who then charged the manager,
Tom Phillips, twopence a length. When this happened we
do not know but Chetwood had returned to Dublin in 1741
after being some years in London, and in 1743 Phillips led a
break-away group of actors from the Smock Alley Company
to establish a little theatre in Capel Street. It seems likely,
then, that Whitley got his first job in the 1741/2 season.
Some time later Chetwood offered the post of prompter's
call boy to Whitley, who took it on being promised by Chetwood that he would train him as an actor. Whitley was still
serving the solicitor, who was still in gaol, but when the
Smock Alley Company went on their usual summer tour he

45

decided to desert his old master and go with them. He was committed at last.

According to Lewes his salary, when paid, was to be seven shillings a week and the first town they went to was Waterford, where they played in a theatre within the Friary, 'a privileged place'. But after nine weeks, though he had made good progress, Whitley had only received seventeen shillings and fivepence in salary, so it was little wonder that he accepted the invitation of the widow Cassandra Parker to join her company at Galway 'with a pleasing offer of a first cast of parts'. He took with him, in lieu of salary, a considerable number of playbooks belonging to the Smock Alley company, all 'well cut, marked and margined' by Chetwood, and 'made his first appearance in The Cure for a Scold compiled from Shakespeare's play of that name'.[85] Later that season he married the widow Parker and became joint manager of the company; he was then eighteen and she twenty-six, says Lewes, so this may have been late in the year 1742 or early '43. The company attracted only poor audiences and Whitley told Lewes that in these days he and his wife suffered great poverty and 'lived many days upon bread and buttermilk in the plentiful town of Carlow'; many of the players left them (Havard for one, to appear in Dublin in 1743) and finally the Whitleys decided to sell up everything and try their fortunes in England. They arrived at Liverpool, where they were made welcome by John Heron whose company was playing there. This is the same manager whose playbills for *The Recruiting Officer* and *The Fair Penitent* 'At the Exchange' in Manchester are in the Central Library collection and have been marked '1743'; the one for the Fair Penitent is torn and has the uncompleted lines:

The Part of Sciolto by Mr. W . . .
and the Part of Horatio by Mr. Ma . . .
(from the Theatre Royal in Dub . . .

Could 'Mr. W ...' be Whitley? Sciolto was one of his parts, according to a story told of him by Henry Lee.[86] In the same company were Mr. and Mrs. Stanford: the latter has already been noted as being in Whitley's company at Stamford in 1752. Who was "Mr. Ma ... " from the Theatre Royal in Dublin? Macklin did not go there until 1748.[87] From this time on, says Lewes, Whitley prospered, though he was not yet quite shrewd enough to avoid being dismissed by Heron, who found him towards the end of the season attempting to persuade some of the players to join in a new company with himself as manager. Whitley then joined a band of 'lawless resolutes' who were playing somewhere on the borders of Wales and soon persuaded them to accept him as manager. 'In short', concludes Lewes, 'from this small beginning he rose to a pitch of affluence before unknown to provincial managers'.[88]

Who these 'lawless resolutes' were we do not know. The team which Whitley took over is not traced again until 1750/51 when we hear of them in Leeds where they replaced a company which had been coming over from York.[89] Not only did they give successful performances, says Miss Rosenfeld, but their 'private and public behaviour was especially commended'. Three of the players are named for a performance in aid of the hospital on December 27, 1751: Sherrife, Morgan and Mrs. Wheeler—an early record of this lady's association with Whitley which was to last for at least another twenty-one years. In February, 1752, the company was in Chester and one of the benefit performances was for Miss Adams and Miss J. Adams;[90] in April they had moved to Stamford in Lincolnshire where Mrs. Stanford took a benefit and spoke an Epilogue of Thanks on the 21st which Whitley had reprinted in the *Manchester Mercury*.

The Stamford theatre was associated with Whitley and his family for many years; he probably built the new theatre there in 1768 and at his death bequeathed it, along with the rents of the other theatres he owned, to his daughter who had married a Mr. Gosli, a dancing master in the town; so we find this reference in the Winston manuscript dated July, 1793:

> Theatre the property of Mrs. Gosle [sic] built about 35 Years Robertson (manager). it was recond a wonderfully grand place as before that they playd in barns throughout this part of the Country. It is a pretty Th. now and lately we have much improved it by taking away the Heavy pillars & putting in their place small cast Iron ones. business at Races & fair is very good, principal perfs. well rewarded at their Benf. Charges 11 Guineas. The charges here are law as an equivalent for the performers play—.[91]

The item is headed 'Pero (Manager)': he was Whitley's grandson and succeeded him as manager of the circuit. This family connection with Stamford may have its beginnings in Whitley's days at the Smock Alley Theatre in Dublin where he would naturally have met and talked with many of the players. Two of them at least we know to have had connections with Stamford; Robert Wetherelt, whose parents 'belonged to a country company at Stamford in Lincolnshire',[92] and Mrs. Furnivall, a leading actress in Dublin in the 1740s where she played Queen to Garrick's Hamlet[93] and who later trained Sarah Siddons's father to act. Mrs. Furnivall, according to Lee Lewes, played for Whitley in Stamford and delighted the Cecil family with her excellence.[94]

In the next few years Whitley was building his reputation in the circuit of towns which he later selected as the regular dates for his company; in 1757/8 for example he was once more in Leeds where two puffs in the *Leeds Intelligence* refer to performances in the concert room of the Rose and Crown.[95] In the second one there is reference to 'the profits arising from a benefit given to the poor' being 'nearly equal to those given this year at York'. In the following winter 1759/60 we know that he began his first association with Manchester, and a year later still there is an announcement in the *Leeds Intelligence* which gives some indication of the extent of the empire he had been busily developing for ten years or so:

> We are assured that Mr. Whitley's Company (who from their strict regards to Decency and Morality in their performances as well as Decorum in their private characters have been established on the most natural principles at Manchester, Nottingham, Leicester, Chester, Shrewsbury and other capital places) intend to entertain the Ladies and Gentlemen of this Town and neighbourhood for a part of the ensuing Winter.[96]

To this list we can add Doncaster, where Lee Lewes joined the company for a short time, and Preston.[97] Lewes speaks of him at this time (1760) as having 'arrived at his grand climacteric, grew hypochondrial, and, as is the case with many of his brother misers when they have accumulated wealth, are loth to make their wills which they consider as a forerunner of their speedy dissolution, deferred that act of family duty as long as he could'.[98]

We can ignore the reference to Whitley's health—he was good for another twenty years—and as to his will, when he did make it it was a model for all future managers, as will be seen. But there is a clear indication here that Whitley was already a man of wealth and power in the theatrical world, and Lewes had already had a taste of the manager's high opinion of himself:

> At the rehearsal in the morning Whitley stood before me and after I had repeated the speech asked me significantly if I meant to speak it so. Yes, sir. "Why, my dear, it may do in these companies you have been in, but it won't do with me, my dear."[99]

Yet Whitley was generous in his later treatment of Lewes, and over-ruled his wife who would have dealt harshly with him when it was discovered that Lewes was negotiating to join Herbert's company at Sheffield.[100]

It is possible that by this time Whitley had already begun to invest in the actual building of theatres in towns where previously only barns or inns or concert rooms were available. In an article "Nottingham's first Theatre" in the *Nottingham Weekly Express* of June 1, 1922, Bernard Stevenson says:

> Until the year 1760 Nottingham had no building that could be legitimately described as a theatre yet theatrical performances took place from time to time.
>
> It was left to an Irishman to found Nottingham's first permanent theatre. James Whitley, whom the local historian Blackner described as "the wealthy master of an itinerant company of players" left his mark on the theatrical history of a very large area of the Midlands.

He had also already demonstrated his interest in new plays and playwrights—a very natural and sensible interest, since success with a new play would be a feather in any provincial manager's cap. He had tried his hand at it himself with a play called *The Humbug*[101] and Broadbent reports that when Whitley's company was playing in 'the theatre in the tennis court' at Chester early in 1761, Francis Gentleman first met Whitley and wrote *The Modish Wife;* he then offered this to the manager who 'got the piece up with care: it was very well performed and most kindly received for four nights'.[102]

For the next twenty years Whitley consolidated his circuit, occasionally extended it and occasionally lost one or two towns in the incessant struggle between rival managers which went on all over the country at this time. There is a good example of this in Tate Wilkinson's memoirs. It was in 1763 that Wilkinson first met Whitley and played six or seven nights at Salop at the end of September when he was on his way to Dublin; in June of the following year he played for Whitley again at Chester.[103] Ten years later Wilkinson was himself a manager and boasts of how he won Wakefield from Whitley:

> . . . we had a shabby theatre there but better than the inhabitants of the town had ever been accustomed to. Decent theatres in the country were almost unknown thirty years ago. We had to oppose Mr. Whiteley [sic] that season; however we not only obtained victory, but defeated and routed the enemy . . .[104]

In the following year the actor Powell left Wilkinson's company at York in May.

> . . . on being allured with the idea of getting into managerial power (smelling to one nosegay like the two Kings of Brentford) with Mr. Whiteley [sic] a genius possessed of powers and fame on the theatrical turf. But the connection did not last long: Whiteley would not give up any part of his monarchy, for which Powell thirsted as eagerly as Dives did for a drop of water from Lazarus to cool his tongue.[105]

Powell in fact remained with Whitley only until after the company had finished at Cambridge at the end of September; he then went over to join the Mattocks and Younger Company which in its turn had driven Whitley from Manchester. There was no quarter shown anywhere, the survival of the fittest was the only motto. When Betty Martin, deserted by Elrington in Caernarvon, finally came to the end of her tether as a manager in 1766 she went to Whitley and offered to join his company. Whitley agreed to take her but only on condition that she sold to him all her assets in her own company, which he then promptly disbanded.[106] This is the widow 'Mrs. Workman' (as she had by then become) who appears as a player in his Manchester company that year.

By this time Whitley was all-powerful in the Midlands circuit, with the rents of a number of the theatres securely in his own hands. If we are to believe Henry Lee:

> He was for many years the manager of the principal tours in the Midland Counties: Derby, Nottingham, Northampton, Lincoln, Leicester, etc. I believe Mr. Whiteley [sic] with the exception of myself, built more theatres than any other manager in the Kingdom. But he was more prudent than I have been. Building too was less expensive than it has ever been since: besides Mr. Whiteley had the address to get the public to build theatres for him, and left them under his own direction. Now I have not been blessed with such powers of persuasion: I have all my life been so dull as to build theatres for myself; Mr. Whiteley's plan was much the best.[107]

The Thespian Dictionary credits him with

> . . . the most extensive Midland circuit ever known in England: Worcester, Wolverhampton, Derby, Nottingham, Bedford and Stamford theatres, etc. etc. were his.

About 1770 he appears to have added to his managerial interests by becoming joint manager with Herbert of the East Anglian circuit, with Newark and King's Lynn as its principal centres: the details of the arrangement between the two managers are not known, nor how long the association lasted. It may well have been until Whitley's death in 1781. The earliest known playbills of a new theatre built within St. George's Hall, King's Lynn, in 1766/7 are for 1774 and advertise Whitley and Herbert's company, with Cooke and Miss Glassington as leading players.[108] Whitley's name does not finally disappear from the playbills until 1781. There is a hint of a busy manager having to be in too many places at once in the preliminary paragraph of an advertisement of

Whitley's benefit in the *Nottingham Journal* for August 19, 1775.

> From a consciousness that he has been called from the business of the theatre by unavoidable journeys, and as Mr. Whitley must attend the preparing this masterly production . . .

he begs to be excused from the usual courtesy of calling upon his many supporters in the town. This was for a production of *Henry VIII* in which his grandson Pero played the King and Mrs. McGeorge Queen Katherine. Mr. Whitley sang songs during the evening and then retired happily to the Black Swan which had been his headquarters in Nottingham for many years.

It was in this period also that he became involved in a quarrel with Macklin for performing *Love à la Mode* without that author's permission. So much of this kind of thing was going on that Macklin decided to make an example of Whitley, and wrote to his lawyer on May 18, 1771, enclosing a playbill as evidence of the offence.

> The offender is one Whitley whose christian name I know not. He is the master of a Strolling Company, and generally acts at Manchester, Derby and Leicester so that an acquaintance at any of those places might inform me of his christian name, should it be necessary to the filing of a bill, or, were I to write a letter to him, I suppose that would draw it from him.[109]

In fact Macklin went to Leicester, 'intent on the destruction of the said Whitley', and delivered a written ultimatum. But Macklin was not only ignorant of Whitley's Christian name; he underestimated the manager's skill and astuteness in such matters. Henry Lee says that they actually met and 'got into warm words' on the subject, with Macklin trying to browbeat Whitley by contemptuous references to his lack of education: 'Did you ever read Locke, sir? Locke on Human Understanding?' Whitley rejoined 'that curl of hair

on your forehead is not, sir, I fear, a lock on human understanding'.[110] Whether the story is true or not, and whether
they 'spent the evening in as merry a manner as possible',
there is Whitley's written reply showing how well he under-
stood the niceties of such a situation, his better understanding of the intricacies of the law, his dignity and firmness
when he felt himself and his calling to be insulted.[111] Judge
Parry describes Whitley as 'a clever rogue, having been bred
an attorney' (an interesting reference to the boyhood days
in Dublin) and his letter as 'this bit of transpontine impu-
dence'; it is as well for Parry that he wrote when Whitley
had been dead for just over a hundred years.

The full extent of Whitley's dominions in these last years
of his life is difficult to assess: his drive and energy must
have been extraordinary, and so must his optimism. His disappointment in the loss of the Manchester theatre does not
seem to have deterred him from pressing on with his interests in other towns: he was already well known in Derby
and in 1773, says Procter, ordered the erection of the Derby
theatre in anticipation of the Manchester crisis.[112] In 1776 a
new theatre was opened in Sheffield, where Herbert's company had played on many occasions.[113] The prologue on the
opening night was written by Whitley and spoken by
Payne: another actor, Richards, who was in the Manchester
company from 1770 to 1775 had an uninteresting and vulgar
quarrel there with Whitley about the same time.[114] But
whether Whitley was also instrumental in building the
second theatre we do not know. In 1778 there are references
to a new theatre in Nottingham,[115] which could mean no
more than improvements to the old one which Whitley had
built on the west side of St. Mary's Gate in 1760;[116] the town
was a Whitley stronghold and the advertisements in the
Nottingham Journal show that his company certainly
occupied the improved building.

In the last year of his life this astonishing man was busily extending his control of theatres into the western part of the Midlands, in Worcester and Wolverhampton. Theatrical performances in Worcester can be traced back to 1717 but evidence of regular seasons in the town does not begin until 1755. These performances took place in a timber building which stood in a yard opposite the Guildhall in the High Street, and the managers of visiting companies, among them Roger Kemble, made improvements to it at various times. Early in 1780 Whitley took his company to Worcester for the first time and, having completed certain alterations to the building, announced in the *Worcester Journal* on March 16:

> Our new theatre, which is now better fitted for the reception of a polite audience than ever it was before, was opened on the 8th instant by Mr. Whitley's company.

But clearly he was not satisfied with the place, and so, being very well received by the town, he announced a month later (April 13) a subscription scheme for the erection of a 'new and complete theatre in a most eligible situation'; twelve subscriptions of not less than fifty and not more than a hundred pounds were to be in his hands by May 15 and he offered a five per cent interest. The money was quickly provided, a site in Angel Street chosen and the theatre was opened on March 29, 1781, with a performace of Murphy's *The Grecian Daughter* by 'capital performers from the Theatres Royal in Dublin and Edinburgh'.[117]

Nothing now remains of this building, which served the town for nearly a hundred years but which saw no more of Whitley after the first season. He had been too ill in the autumn of 1780 to appear with his company at Nottingham and was soon to hand over the management of his affairs to his daughter, Mrs. Gosli, and of his circuits to his grandson,

Mr. Pero, and Mrs. Pero, who had been regular members of his company for the last few years. It is somewhat ironic to find him at the age of about fifty-six referred to by Grice in *Theatre Notebook* as one of the 'younger men' who were to benefit from the revival of interest in drama which 'the ageing Kemble' had fostered in Worcester,[118] and dismissed in a later article tracing the history of Whitley's new theatre with 'under the successive managements of Powell and Pero (Whitley soon disappears) ... the theatre continues to flourish'.[119] His death in September, 1781, is the simple explanation: Powell and Pero were his appointed successors, veterans of his company who had learned everything from him.

What sort of a man was Whitley? The stories about him in the memoirs of his brother managers are numerous: some kindly, some contemptuous and one or two like Henry Lee, genuinely admiring. They recall his eccentric, flamboyant mannerisms, his tremendous pride in his profession and his blazing anger whenever anyone criticised unkindly any of his players—*that* particular function was reserved solely to himself as manager, and he showed no mercy to those who challenged his authority or disgraced their calling. Some of the accounts of his behaviour are flavoured with that same mixture of awe and respect with which a schoolboy remembers in later years the master who caned him most but who taught him most.[120] Far above everything else, Whitley asked for loyalty from his players, and he rewarded it handsomely at his death.

Whitley was a great democrat and a great provincial: it may be that he knew, better than anyone else, that he would never be a success in London: but having accepted that, he set for himself high standards of conduct and integrity and was immensely proud of his reputation and his achievements. What the artistic standards of his company were like

it is difficult to say: the managers of those days all boasted
loudly about the superior qualities of their own teams, and
what Macklin or Tate Wilkinson may have to say about
Whitley is not so much evidence as familiar professional
slander. If we are to believe what later observers tell us, the
standards of provincial companies at the turn of the nineteenth century were abysmally low, and it is perhaps sensible
to assume that Whitley's company was no better and no
worse than the average in his time.

Throughout his whole career as manager (about thirty-
eight years) he was never once gaoled for debt, and was
never, so far as we know, in serious trouble with the authorities. This is something of an achievement for a provincial
theatre manager in the eighteenth century, particularly for
one who never assumed for his company the protective titles
'From the Theatres Royal' or 'His Majesty's Servants', as so
many other managers did. Whitley's company, if he described it at all, was always 'Comedians from the Theatres'.

We know little or nothing of his private and family life.
When he married Cassandra Parker she had, according to
Lee Lewes, two children and it is not known whether the
daughter Betsy who became a player in his company was one
of these or was Whitley's own child. Mrs. Whitley played
parts in the earlier years but does not appear on the playbills
after about 1760: Lee Lewes gives the impression that she
was something of a tyrant with the other players. She was
eight years older than Whitley and probably died before
him, since she is not mentioned in his will.

A season had been advertised in Nottingham to com-
mence on August 2, 1781, but was postponed for some
reason; then, at the beginning of September Whitley came
for the first time to Wolverhampton and died there on September 13.[121] He was then probably in his fifty-seventh year.
He is buried at Wolverhampton. The cause of his death is

unknown. The Whitley family assumed the responsibilities of the business and the postponed Nottingham season opened on October 22 with O'Brien managing the company on behalf of Whitley's daughter, Mrs. Gosli, and with George Frederick Cooke in the company.

Whitley died comfortably off—in itself a rare tribute to his abilities as manager—and left the rents of his theatres 'to the amount of nearly £500 per annum'[123] and the management of his circuit to his daughter. But his will contains a most remarkably generous bequest to those of his veteran performers who survived him, a commendation of them to his successors with a weekly salary entailed on them for life, 'which those who still survive continue to enjoy—an example worthy of imitation!'[123]

Whitley had done more for the provincial theatre in England, both in 'bricks and mortar' and in skilful management, than any manager before him. And at the time the fact was widely recognized.

The name and fame of this person pervaded the three Kingdoms and a hundred recollections of his personal and managerial peculiarities are now thronging my head.[124]

A man of very singular disposition and to whom more whimsical and out of the way exertions are imputed than to any other manager or country actor in the British territory—the eccentricity of his disposition brought him often into strange situations, but the goodness of his heart fully atoned for the errors of his understanding: and however marvellous or irregular some of his actions might appear he perpetrated others of a nature so dignified that they would have done honour to the possessor of a national throne.[125]

While I was at Wolverhampton I occasionally used to meditate among the tombs in the churchyard, especially over the grave of Mr. Whiteley [sic], the manager who is spoken of in another place. He was buried in or near this church porch, and if I forget not, lies without a stone or inscription to his memory.

This is to be lamented, because he was certainly a man of original talent; many droll jokes and whimsical incidents that have delighted the public in modern dramas had their origin in the facetious brain of this eccentric man. Had London been the circle in which he moved, instead of the country, he would have made some figure in dramatic history. He subscribed himself James Augustus Whitley.[126]

IV

THE REPERTORY

It is time to return to Manchester and complete the story of the Marsden Street theatre. For the next nine consecutive seasons from 1766 Whitley was the sole provider of plays, with a stock company whose principal members had not, apart from his own family, been in Manchester with him on his last visit in 1760–61. Kniveton and King led the men in the first season, Mrs. Wheeler and Mrs. Williams the ladies, with Betty Martin ("Mrs. Workman") strongly supporting.

During these nine seasons many of the same names appear on the playbills year after year; there was clearly a strong loyalty to Whitley within his company. He employed about twenty-five players during most of his Manchester seasons, though on two occasions he had as many as thirty-two. Some of these would be local players who joined him when he arrived; one of them was Ward, a local printer who afterwards was manager for many years of the second Theatre Royal in Fountain Street. It is possible that Dunn and Peters (who all played every season with him) were also local.

These provincial companies were an excellent training ground for young actors and actresses, and London managers frequently sent their agents to search for new talent among them. The most quoted example is Garrick's letter to Moody at Liverpool in 1776: 'Have you heard of a woman Siddons who is strolling about somewhere near you?' She was there, all right. One such young actress, who later shared the honours with Mrs. Siddons at Drury Lane, was with Whitley in the 1773–74 season; this was Elizabeth Farren, whom Walpole was to describe as the most perfect actress he had ever seen, and who in 1797 became Lady Derby.

It would not be of any great value to the reader if we were to go through each of Whitley's seasons from 1766 to 1775 in detail; the typescript schedules in the Manchester Central Library give the plays, players, times and prices as shown in the press advertisements or such playbills as exist; the card index of plays gives the dates when each was performed as far as we know them; the list of actors and actresses tells us when they appeared in Manchester and for which manager; and the 'Items of Special Interest' in each schedule add flavour to all these cold facts, incomplete though they are. These are all available for consultation by any one wishing to study the provincial theatre in all its detail. We shall therefore comment only on the more significant features of these last nine years.

Whitley began prudently, as always; he did the minimum of newspaper advertising in his first two seasons, announcing only the Wednesday performances (i.e. the day following the publication of the *Mercury*) and afterwards waiting for the benefits to start and so letting his players spread themselves in the Press, at their own expense. This is our loss today; only a few of the playbills in the Central Library cover the many gaps in the complete repertoire. He also declined to spend money on the 'Italian' dancers, who had been a feature of the visits by the London companies; there are no Fabianos and Tassonis in Whitley's seasons. His programmes were straightforward stock repertory with the play followed by a farce, and though in his selection of plays he relied mainly on old favourites and a plentiful supply of farces, he continued to show initiative in bringing new plays each season. In November, 1767, he staged Francklin's *The Earl of Warwick*, which had appeared for the first time at Drury Lane the previous winter; the next year he gave Murphy's *Zenobia* within nine months of its London première; in the 1772–73 season there were at least four such Manchester premières, and in 1773–74 there were at least five. Among these was the first performance in Manchester of *She Stoops To Conquer*; it was given in the December following the first London presentation the previous March. In the last season (1775) came *The Rivals*, only three months after its first night at Covent Garden.

Whether Whitley was able to give the author's text of these plays or only some agent's version it is impossible to tell. There was no copyright in those days and one of the problems of a manager with a new successful play was to prevent copies getting into the hands of other managers, or their agents sneaking into his theatre to note the principal incidents and speeches and then create their own versions. John Wilks gives an illuminating description of how this was done when he was employed by Ryder in Dublin some years later:

> I embarked for England to engage Mrs. Barry and being on the spot I endeavoured to procure a copy of The School for Scandal—the play had been brought out that season.
>
> Mr. Ryder had played The Duenna under some fears, for altho' he altered the title to The Governess a Lawsuit was taken against him by Mr. Brinsley Sheridan, but did not succeed. Mr. Ryder particularly applied to me to request a copy of The School for Scandal, and for that purpose to apply to Mr. Gurney, which I did, and several other of the shorthand writers in London but not one would undertake the task of writing the play from the performance. So some of my friends and I absolutely set about the labour and completed it almost literally, with the song and epilogue.
>
> The mode we took was by going into the two-shilling gallery

a party of five. By sitting together, two on one seat, two behind and one below, we composed a group and with paper and pencils each writing down the direct words of one of the characters in a scene and regulating the whole in a committee after each performance, in four or five nights we completed the whole.

When I returned I gave it to Mr. Ryder who was to pay me for my expenses to London and the cash and expenses on the business £40 which I unfortunately never received.[127]

It was because of this sort of thing that established authors like Sheridan frequently released their plays as soon as they could in order to protect their own reputation. Sheridan knew that it would be impossible to prevent his favourite comedy from being acted in Ireland:

therefore he made a merit of necessity and sent a copy to his sister who, I was told, received £100 for the manuscript. The difference in the two copies was very trifling, the fair and the pirated, but we performed it from the original one.[128]

The Manchester Theatre, being a non-patent theatre, is unlikely to have been given the first offer of the scripts of new London successes, but Whitley obviously did his best to keep his patrons up to date and his business thriving. This sometimes got him into trouble, as it did with Macklin in 1771 over *Love à la Mode*.

The plays of Shakespeare, or rather the versions which were typical of this period, were presented regularly each season; *Henry IV* and *The Merry Wives* were staunch favourites, so were *The Merchant of Venice* and *As You Like It*. Among the tragedies *Hamlet*, *Romeo and Juliet*, and *King Lear* came most often, and of the histories there was nothing to rival *Richard III*. *The Tempest* was presented as 'an opera, altered by Dryden' and of the other plays *Cymbeline*, curiously enough, appears most frequently —but in Garrick's version.

The other authors whose plays were most popular were Garrick, Fielding, Samuel Foote, Arthur Murphy, for contemporary comedies and farces, with Colley Cibber and Farquhar to represent classical (i.e. Restoration) comedy. The emphasis is definitely on comedy though tragedies like James Thomson's *Tancred and Sigismunda*, Otway's *The Orphan*, and Rowe's *Tamerlaine the Great* were constantly appearing.

It seems as though Whitley's return to Manchester in 1766 was not to everybody's delight; his was not a 'No. 1 Company'—as we say today—and there must have been many people who thought that the town deserved better and ought to have nothing less than 'His Majesty's Servants' to play to them. Whitley was obviously answering these criticisms when he sent his daughter Betsey on to the stage in December, 1766, to speak these lines 'with great applause, to polite Audiences':

This well lov'd Stage I once more tread
This Audience View, whom I revere and dread;
Since I have heard each specious little Art,
Each sly, collusive, undermining Part
Has been employ'd to hurt our Station here,
That others may supplant us in a Year,
While we with Patience have one Point in View,
The hope, with modest Toil, to pleasure you:
Involuntary Errors Pity Claim,
The Balm Compassion cures the Canker Blame.
If warmest Gratitude for Favours Past,
And eager hopes they will not be the last,
Of Promptitude to please, with gen'rous Minds,
As heretofore, a kind Reception finds;
If reverential Awe and Homage true
Are Debts we thus acknowledge due to you,
No Cost, no Application shall we spare
Your Favour and Encouragement to share.
Tho' not from LONDON, many Actors here
Well worthy of Applause may yet appear,

On just examination you will find
Desert to no one Station is consigned:
Why may not MANCHESTER with Cities vie
For Judgment, and the Powers to descry
Comedians Faults, or their Perfections own,
Since well for Science as for Commerce known?
Shall proud AUGUSTA or shall DUBLIN claim
Sole Privilege to fix an Actor's Fame?
O no, my friends—Assert your Freeborn Task
Judge for yourselves, 'tis *that* we humbly ask,
Banish Chagrin for Sounds subjoin'd to Sense,
And be as fam'd for Taste as Opulence,
Then Candour shall from ev'ry Terror raise us
And as you prove us, condescend to praise us.[129]

Note the appeal to Manchester to have a mind of its own
instead of submitting to 'Proud Augusta's'. It is a piece of
good, hard hitting at critics and detractors, and if Betsey
was a true daughter of her enterprising father she must have
roused the audience to fine effect that night.

Gradually Whitley appears to have overcome the prejudice against his company, at least for a time, and to have
improved conditions in the House. In the 1769–70 season
he increased the prices from the usual two shillings and one
shilling by introducing boxes for the first time, and charging
three shillings, for a seat in them. These boxes were probably
no more than the usual partitioning off of the front of the
gallery and upper gallery (upper boxes two shillings) so
that patrons who desired could be segregated from the
crowd. They also had the privilege of being burned or
crushed to death in fires, panics, or riots, since they could
never open the box doors when such disasters occurred because of the terrified crowds outside. But Whitley suffered
no catastrophies; though he announced in January, 1768
'There will be stoves to warm the Pit' no fires broke out,
and never at any time is there any suggestion of panics or
riots. This says much for Whitley and for Manchester

audiences; in 1778 they were for tearing the Theatre Royal to pieces in Liverpool because Younger dared to present a company (including Mrs. Siddons) which had not appeared before the King.

A playbill preserved in the Central Library reveals that on the Monday after the 1769–70 season ended (March 5, 1770) Whitley's company gave a performance of *The Jealous Wife* and *The Padlock* for the Benefit of The Infirmary—best proof that Whitley was accepted in Manchester. By 1771–72 he was even more sure of himself; his company was larger than it had ever been and he stayed for a longer season (eighteen weeks). In 1773–74 he came for twenty-one weeks; this was the season when Elizabeth Farren joined him and he introduced so many plays for the first time in Manchester.[130]

He had already shown his willingness also to encourage local writers (e.g. on February 8, and March 1, 1773, when both plays were announced as having been written by "a gentleman of Manchester"); unfortunately an additional reference by Axon to *Codrus,* a tragedy by Dorning Ramsbottom, J.P., which was performed once at the Theatre Royal and afterwards printed, cannot be traced in the records of Whitley's company for the year given by Axon (1774) but it was certainly printed.[131] Each year he had been coming later and later to the town and so playing more into the spring; in 1773 he did not open until December 8 and his next season (the last) was delayed until January 9, 1775. The reasons for the delay may be that this was the year in which he joined up with Herbert in King's Lynn; or may be connected in some way with an announcement in the *Mercury* for November 15, 1774:

It having been industriously reported, that many of the performers belonging to this Theatre, are engaged to perform with the Company who propose playing at Manchester this season, I hereby assure the Public that I am authorised by my Performers in general to declare that no one of them is either engaged or in treaty to play in Manchester in the present Theatre.

JOSEPH YOUNGER

This was not the first shot which had been fired by the Liverpool manager in his battle to win Manchester for his company. On September 18, 1774, he inserted a notice in the *Mercury* of his own benefit performance at the Theatre Royal in *Liverpool* the following Friday. This was clearly intended to impress any friends in Manchester who were supporting the proposal for a Theatre Royal in their town, and to disassociate himself from the present theatre i.e., the non-patent theatre. There were probably many such who recalled that Liverpool had been granted a Royal Patent in 1771 and were eager for the same recognition in Manchester.

We have not discovered when the project for a new theatre first began, nor when actual building commenced. It must have been almost completed when the 'Bill to enable His Majesty to license a Playhouse in the Town of Manchester' was debated in Parliament in 1775 and was finally passed.[132]

But this is anticipating; Whitley was not done yet. Indeed he showed remarkable determination and fought back very handsomely. On January 3, 1775, he announced in the *Mercury* his return to Manchester, thanked all his numerous friends and issued a 'Proposal for a Subscription'. This would enable patrons to secure a seat for twenty-one nights at the theatre at a cost of £1 11s. 6d. for the boxes, and £1 1s. for the pit and upper boxes—half price in fact. They would see one of Shakespeare's plays every Monday, and the company would 'at a week's notice, get up any piece that ten or more subscribers shall appoint, the characters to be cast agreeable to their request'. In addition they would see a 'House new

Ornamented, the Boxes secured from Cold by Curtains, and illuminated with Wax'—and if subscribers were still not satisfied after three nights they could have their money back.

The season opened on Monday, January 9, with *The Merchant of Venice*, and lasted for nineteen weeks; many of the performances were 'by desire' of some local influential society, one or two with remarkable names like 'Knights Companion of the Most Noble Order of the Beggars Bennison'. Many of the plays presented were once again new to Manchester (e.g. *The Rivals*) or had 'not been seen these twenty years' (*Julius Caesar*).

Whether the subscription scheme was successful we cannot say, but Shakespeare was *not* presented every Monday, and the first announcement about wax does not come until the eleventh week. We know now that Whitley lost the battle and retired from the Manchester Theatre for good on May 12. We have traced him and most of his company later that year (August) in Nottingham[133] and he continued busily in the provincial theatres until his death six years later. One of the most loyal and regular members of his company, Mr. Wheeler, later went off to try his fortune in Dublin, but does not appear to have had much luck.[134]

The Theatre Royal in Manchester, however, was for Younger, who brought a company over from Liverpool for a single performance of *Othello* on Whit Monday, June 5, and announced that the theatre would officially open on Monday, October 9.

NOTES

1. *The Journeys of Celia Fiennes,* ed. Christopher Morris, 1947, pp. 223–224.
2. *An enumeration of the Houses and Inhabitants in the Town and Parish of Manchester,* 1778.
3. Everyman edn., 1948, vol. ii, p. 261.
4. E. K. Chambers, *William Shakespeare,* 1930, vol. i, p. 538; Sidney Lee, *William Shakespeare,* 1898, p. 266 (1931 edn.).
5. John Hollinworth, *Chronicle of Manchester,* 1656, p. 75 (1839 edn.).
6. Apr. 12, 1549. (See John Dover Wilson, *Life in Shakespeare's England,* 1910, p. 47 (Pelican edn.).
7. Vol. i, pp. 174–181.
8. Vol. ii, pp. 414, 507.
9. *Manchester Mercury* (subsequently cited as 'the *Mercury*'), Sep. 29, 1761.
10. R. J. Broadbent, *Annals of the Manchester Stage,* 1735–1844, unpublished, typescript in Manchester Central Reference Library, bound in 3 vols., written after the publication of Broadbent's *Annals of the Liverpool Stage* in 1908: vol. i, p. 2.
11. R. W. Procter, *Memorials of Bygone Manchester,* 1880, p. 66 *et seq.*
12. Broadbent, *Manchester Stage,* vol. i, p. 2. The prologue and epilogue of *Anna Bullen* are in Chetham's Library, Manchester. The play was first presented at the Duke's Theatre in Dorset Garden, Apr., 1682.
13. *Mercury,* various dates 1755–60.
14. *Mercury,* Nov. 21, 1752.
15. Procter, *Memorials,* p. 65.
16. Joseph Aston, *The Manchester Guide,* 1804, p. 233 *et seq.*
17. Broadbent, *Manchester Stage,* vol. i, p. 46.
18. See John Berry's map of Manchester.
19. Thomas Snagg, *Recollections of Occurrences,* 1951, pp. 21, 24. The theatre was not then, or ever, entitled to be called Theatre Royal.
20. Aston, *Guide,* p. 233 *et seq.*
21. R. W. Procter, *Manchester in Holiday Dress,* 1866, first published as articles in the *Manchester Guardian* in 1864.
22. Manchester Notes and Queries, vol. vi, May 2, 1885.
23. Broadbent, *Manchester Stage,* vol. i, p. 136.
24. *Mercury,* Mar. 4, 1760.
25. *Mercury,* Mar. 30, 1758.
26. Charles Lee Lewes, *Memoirs,* 1805, vol. i, p. 136.
27. Elizabeth Raffald, *Directory of Manchester,* 1772.
28. *Mercury,* Mar. 25, 1788.
29. Procter, *Memorials,* p. 66 *et seq.*
30. Broadbent, *Manchester Stage,* vol. i, p. 3.

31. Manchester Notes and Queries, vol. vii, July 7, 14, 1888.
32. Composer of the hymn tune universally associated with 'Christians Awake'.
33. Thomas Snagg, an actor who had played in Manchester, describes the situation in his *Recollections*, p. 109. 'The manner of taking a town is by application to the Magistrate or Mayor of the place, which if he listens to, his answer generally is "if I find your Company regular and orderly I shall not take notice of it" . . . As there are specific Acts of Parliament against strolling players a Justice cannot give his permission, tho' in many towns the theatres belong to the Corporation, or the Town Hall is let for hire'.
34. Lewes, *Memoirs,* vol. i, pp. 130–144.
35. *Mercury,* Feb., 1758.
36. Procter, *Manchester in Holiday Dress*, p. 13.
37. Was it bought by Horton? (See p. 15.)
38. *Mercury,* Mar. 17.
39. *Mercury,* May 26.
40. *Mercury,* Feb. 13.
41. *Mercury,* Aug. 31.
42. *Mercury,* Nov. 9.
43. Procter, *Memorials*, p. 66 *et seq.*
44. *Ibid.*
45. *Mercury,* Apr. 29, 1760.
46. Aston, *Guide*, p. 233.
47. *Mercury,* May 5, 1752.
48. *Mercury,* June 3, 1760.
49. *Mercury,* June 10, 1760.
50. *Mercury,* Oct. 21, 1760.
51. *Mercury,* Dec. 23, 1760.
52. W. E. A. Axon, *Annals of Manchester*, 1886, under note of death of John Wheeler in 1789.
53. *Mercury,* Jan. 20, 1761.
54. *Mercury,* Mar. 3, 1761.
55. Robert Hitchcock, *An Historical View of The Irish Stage,* 1788–1794, vol. ii, p. 13.
56. *Mercury,* Oct. 28, 1760.
57. *Mercury,* Nov. 4, 1760.
58. *Mercury,* Jan. 19, 26, 1762.
59. Broadbent, *Manchester Stage,* vol. i, p. 9; F. A. Bruton, *History of Manchester and Salford*, 1924, p. 143; Axon, *Annals*, under date 1761.
60. Bruton, *History*, p. 143.
61. *Mercury,* Feb. 16, 1762.
62. *Mercury,* June 8, 1762.
63. *Mercury,* June 9, 1762.
64. *Mercury,* Aug. 31, 1762.
65. *Mercury,* Aug. 27, 1762.

66. *Mercury*, Sep. 9, 1762.
67. Ed. J. P. Earwaker, 1893, vol. iii.
68. *Mercury*, Aug. 30, 1763.
69. *Mercury*, Dec. 6, 1763.
70. *Mercury*, Aug. 23, 1763.
71. Mrs. Frances Sheridan, *The Discovery*, Drury Lane, Feb. 2; George Colman, *The Deuce is in Him*, D. L., Nov. 4.
72. Vol. iii, p. 67, *et seq.*
73. Snagg, *Recollections*, p. 105.
74. *Ibid.*
75. *Mercury*, June 5, 1764.
76. *Mercury*, June 20, 1764.
77. Snagg, *Recollections*, p. 23.
78. *Ibid.*, pp. 24, 25.
79. *Mercury*, Oct. 16, 1764.
80. Snagg, *Recollections*, pp. 33, 34, 107 (note).
81. *Mercury*, July 23, 1765.
82. Snagg, *Recollections*, p. 34.
83. *Mercury*, Dec. 10, 1765.
84. Lewes, *Memoirs*, vol. i, p. 33 *et seq.*
85. A version of *The Taming of the Shrew*.
86. Henry Lee, *Memoirs of a Manager*, 1830, vol. ii, p. 124.
87. E. A. Parry, *Charles Macklin*, 1891, p. 105.
88. *Memoirs*, p. 45.
89. Sybil Rosenfeld, *Strolling Players and Drama in the Provinces, 1660–1765*, 1939, p. 141.
90. R. J. Broadbent, *Annals of the Chester Stage*, p. 18. Typescript in Liverpool Public Library. There was a Miss Adams in Whitley's Manchester company in the 1768, 1769 seasons.
91. *Theatre Notebook*, 1947, vol. i, p. 93.
92. Hitchcock, *Irish Stage*, p. 95.
93. *Ibid.*, pp. 109-161.
94. *Memoirs*, p. 87.
95. Nov. 15, 1757, Feb. 7, 1758.
96. Oct. 16, 1761.
97. *Mercury*, June 10, 1760.
98. *Memoirs*, pp. 50, 51.
99. *Ibid.*, p. 46.
100. *Ibid.*, p. 58.
101. Described by Nicoll (*Late Eighteenth Century Drama*, p. 315) as *The Intriguing Footman; or the Humours of Harry Humbug*.
102. Broadbent, *Chester Stage*, p. 29.
103. Tate Wilkinson, *Memoirs*, 1791, vol. iii, pp. 162, 232.
104. Tate Wilkinson, *The Wandering Patentee* 1795, vol. i, p. 200.
105. Ibid. vol. i, p. 36.
106. Lewes, *Memoirs*, p. 175.
107. Lee, *Memoirs*, vol. ii, p. 105.
108. *Theatre Notebook*, 1949, vol. iii, p. 25.

109. Parry, *Macklin*, p. 143.
110. Lee, *Memoirs*, vol. ii, p. 133.
111. Parry, *Macklin*, p. 143.
112. Procter, *Manchester in Holiday Dress*, p. 27.
113. Undated playbills in Sheffield Library.
114. Winston Ms., Birmingham Library.
115. *Nottingham Journal*, Aug. 1, 1778.
116. E. Radford, 'Rollicking Nights', *Nottingham Evening News,* Jan. 6, 1920.
117. F. Grice, 'The Theatre Royal at Worcester', *Theatre Notebook,* 1956, vol. x, p. 84.
118. *Theatre Notebook,* 1955, vol. ix, p. 75.
119. *Theatre Notebook,* 1956, vol. x, p. 85.
120. John Bernard, *Retrospections of the Stage,* 1830, vol. i, pp. 155–164; Lee, *Memoirs*, vol. ii, p. 105, 120–124, 133, 147; Anthony Pasquin, *Eccentricities of John Edwin,* 1791, pp. 133-145; Lewes, *Memoirs*, pp. 46–59; Tate Wilkinson, *Memoirs*, vol. iii, p. 126 *et seq*, 232; *Thespian Dictionary,* 1805.
121. *Nottingham Journal*, Sep. 22, 1781.
122. *Thespian Dictionary.*
123. *Ibid.*
124. Bernard, *Retrospections*, vol. i, p. 155.
125. Pasquin, *Eccentricities*, p. 133.
126. Lee, *Memoirs*, vol. i, p. 172.
127. Snagg, *Recollections*, p. 98.
128. *Ibid.*, p. 98.
129. *Mercury*, Dec. 16, 1766.
130. Goldsmith, *She Stoops to Conquer;* Francis Gentleman, *The Pantheonites;* Hull, *Henry the Second;* Charles Dibdin, *The Deserter*; Otway, *Venice Preserv'd.*
131. Axon, *Annals*, under 1774; Nicoll, *Late Eighteenth Century Drama*, p. 322.
132. May 4, 1775. See Earwaker's *Local Gleanings,* vol. iii, p. 311, for text.
133. *Nottingham Journal*, Aug. 19, 1775.
134. Snagg, *Recollections*, p. 96.

Black Friars Bridge, from a lithograph published in 1823

At the EXCHANGE,

MONDAY the 9th *Inftant*, will be acted,

A diverting COMEDY, call'd

THE

RECRUITING OFFICER.

Capt. Plume			Mr. Lewis,
Capt. Brazen			Mr. O'Brian,
Ballance			Mr. Warriner,
Worthy	By		Mr. Stanford,
Kite			Mr. Prigmore,
Bullock			Mr. Heron,
Recruit			Mr. Dale.
Silvia			Mrs. Prigmore,
Melinda	By		Mrs. Lewis,
Rofe			Mrs. Stanford,
Lucy			Mrs. Heron.

To which will be added, a *Pantomime Entertainment* call'd

HARLEQUIN's VAGARIES.

PIT 18d. GALLERY 1s.

To prevent *Complaints* or *Inconvenience* from late HOURS, we are determined to begin punctually AT SIX o'CLOCK.
TICKETS to be had at the *Old Coffee-Houfe*, R. *Whitworth's*,
Bookfeller, next the *Angel-Inn*, Mr. *Bradbury's*, Linnen-Dra-
per and Glover, and at Mr. *Heron's* Lodgings, at Mrs. *War-
minghom's*, Haberdafher, near the *Exchange.*
☞ No *Perfon* to be admitted behind the SCENES, at any Time during the Play.

Playbill, the Exchange, (?) 1743

The first Exchange, 1729–92

The Marsden Street Theatre, from a drawing collected by R. J. Broadbent
for the unpublished *Annals of the Manchester Stage*

By his Majefty's Servants from the Theatres - Royal.

At the THEATRE in MANCHESTER,

On FRIDAY, the 19th of *July*, will be performed,

The London Merchant;

Or, the HISTORY of

George Barnwell.

Barnwell,		Mr. Griffith.	Blunt,			Mr. Waldron.
Trueman,		Mr. Kaefberry.				
Thorowgood,	by	Mr. Fowler.	Milwood,		by	Mrs. Lee.
Uncle,		Mr. Wilkes.	Maria,			Mifs Weftray.
			Lucy,			Mifs Matthews.

End of Act the 1ft, a SONG, by Mrs. *Baddeley*.

To which will be added (for the firft Time) a Pantomime Entertainment, call'd

The Royal Hunters.

OR, THE

Execution of Harlequin.

With Variety of new Decorations, and Scenes painted by Mr. *Williams*.

Harlequin,		Mr. Wright.	Cook,			Mr. Watts.
Clodpole (the Clown)	by	Mr. Haughton.	Pyewoman,		by	Mr. Fowler.
Pantaloon,		Mr. Taffoni.				
Spaniard,		Mr. Waldron.	Colombine,			Mifs Tetley.

HUNTERS, by Mr. Kaefberry, Mr. Wilkes, and Mr. Edwin.

HUNTRESSES, by Mrs. Baddeley, Mifs Weftray, and Mrs. Taffoni.

NUNS, by Mifs Hart and Mifs Matthews.

No Admittance behind the Scenes.

PIT Two Shillings. GALLERY, One Shilling.

The Doors to be open'd at fix, and begin precifely at feven o'Clock.

Tickets to be had at the Old and Crompton's Coffee rooms, at the Bull's Head Inn; at J. Harrop's Bookfeller, and at the King's-Head, in Salford.

Playbill, the Marsden Street Theatre, 1765

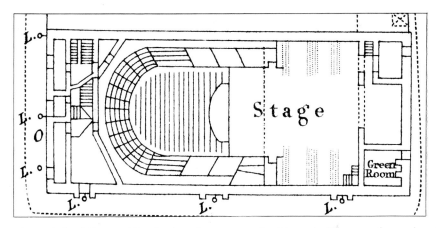

Plan of the Theatre Royal, then known as the Queen's Theatre, from the Ordnance Survey, 1849

The Theatre Royal, from *The Theatric Tourist*, 1805

" *Care to our Coffin adds a Nail—No Doubt!*
" *And every Grin, fo merry, draws One out.*"

THEATRE-ROYAL, MANCHESTER.

On Wednefday the 30th of October, 1793, will be prefented,
THAT MUCH-ADMIRED PRODUCTION OF

NEW BROOMS.

(Confifting of RECITATIONS and Original SONGS)
In THREE PARTS—Written, Selected, and to be Spoken and Sung

BY MR. RYLEY.

PART FIRST.

A New Satirical Prologue—Introductory Comic Song—The Alderman Anatomized—The Poet Pauperized—
The Nabob Analized—The Lawyer Tipified—The Client Stripified—The Bailiff Beautified—
The Kitchen Politician—The Nafal Chorifter;

SIGNOR SQUALINI,

With the ftriking Effects of a Difcord on the Mufcles of a MUSIC MASTER;
To conclude with an IMITATION of
ITALIAN SINGING—BALLAD SINGING—AND SOL FA SINGING.

PART SECOND.

John Bull's Brilliancy Difplayed,

In a Humourous DIALOGUE on the Subject of LIBERTY, SLAVERY, and RELIGION,
between a POOR PRISONER, a PORTER, and a VETERAN.

THE SCIENTIFIC CONTRAST,

Or BUTTERFLY-HUNTING and COMET-CATCHING;

A TREATISE on TURN COATS;

In which will be exhibited,
The Prattling Politician, feized with the LOCK JAW.

A ftriking Likenefs of GENERAL DUMOURIER, from the Original, taken when he was in London;
With an entire new COMIC SONG, called,

BULLY COCK's BOAST;

Or, DUMOURIER's Ducking in the Waters of WILLIAMSTADT.

A SATIRE on ACTING.

To conclude with the Comic Song called the JOKE

PART THIRD.

DOCTOR DISMAL; SOLOMON SADTIMES; JOHN BULL;
With a NEW COMIC SONG, called

THE HOUSE THAT JACK BUILT.

Falfe Bottoms exemplified in TIPPOO SAIB, an Highwayman, and a Lottery-Office-Keeper.
Matrimony Diffected, or a True Pattern of Conjugal Felicity—The Old Maid—The Life and Death of
PEGGY BANN, with a New Pathetic Ballad—The Good Woman—The French
Dancing Mafter—The Old Soldier.

BUMPKIN ENLISTED; with a Comic Song, call'd,

THE DRILLED RECRUIT.

The whole to conclude with a whimfical Defcription and Imitation of

THE LOYAL TAILORS.

Boxes 3s.—Pit 2s—Gallery 1s.

☞ The Doors to be opened at Six, and the Performance to begin at Seven.
Tickets to be had of Mr. Harrop, Printer; the Bridgewater Arms; the Swan; and of Mr. **Ryley**, at
Mr. Andrews. Joiner, Bottom of Fountain-ftreet, oppofite the Brufhmaker's Arms.
Boxes to be taken of Mr. Ryley, and of Mr. Green, at the Theatre.

Playbill, The Theatre Royal, 1793

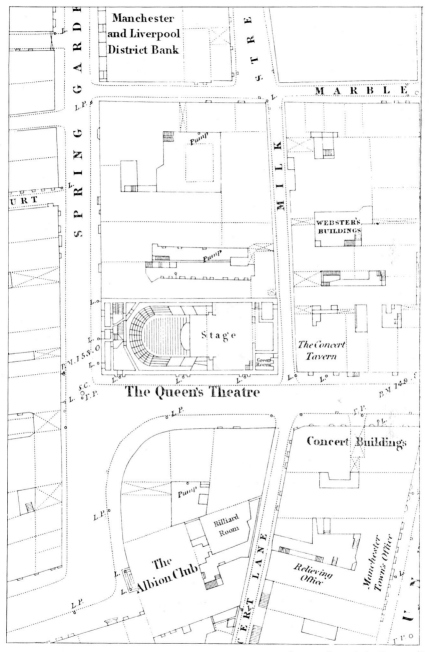

Street Plan, from the Ordnance Survey, 1849

THIS PRESENT FRIDAY.
Mrs. SIDDONS's NIGHT.
And POSITIVELY the LAST TIME of Her PERFORMING this
SEASON.

THEATRE-ROYAL, MANCHESTER.

THIS EVENING November 22d, 1793, will be prefented the TRAGEDY, of

Venice Preferv'd.

Jaffier,   Mr.   C O O K E
Pierre,   Mr.   B A N K S
Renault,   Mr.   T Y R R E L L
Priuli,   Mr.   D A V I S
Bedamar,   Mr.   W I L L I A M S O N
Duke,   Mr.   H A T T O N
Elliot,   Mr.   R O B E R T S
Spinofa,   Mr.   T A Y L O R.
Theodore,   Mr.   Q U A N T R E L L
Officer,   Mr.   K I N G

The Part of Belvidera,   Mrs.   S I D D O N S

To which will be added a FARCE, called

TheAdventurers.

Sir Perigrine Bramble,   Mr.   D A V I S
Metaphor,   Mr.   T A Y L O R
Perigrine Bramble,   Mr.   H A T T O N
Lord Gleanwell,   Mr.   R O B E R T S.
Peter,   Mr.   K I N G
Landlord,   Mr.   Q U A N T R E L L

Lady Bramble,   Mrs.   P O W E L L
Harriet Bramble,   Mrs.   A R N O L D.
Kitty,   Mifs   V A L O I S.

Doors to be opened at SIX, the Curtain to rife precifely at SEVEN o'Clock.

Tickets and Places to be had of Mr. GREEN, at the Front of the Theatre from TEN to ONE o'Clock.

Ladies and Gentlemen who wifh for Places, are requefted to afcertain the exact Number, and defire their Servants to take Tickets at the fame time.

According to the Regulation of all Theatres-Royal, Places cannot be kept longer than the Firft Act of the Play.

Servants to attend to keep Places at half after five o'Clock.

Playbill, the Theatre Royal, 1793

THE FIRST THEATRE ROYAL
1775—1807
by Rex Pogson

I

1775—1781

A BILL to enable the king to license a playhouse in Manchester was introduced in the House of Lords on May 4, 1775, by Lord Lyttelton. It was passed, but not without opposition, notably from the Earl of Radnor, who had strenuously fought a similar bill for Liverpool a few years earlier. The customary fears that the working classes would be seduced from their labours, and their morals corrupted by such plays as *The Beggar's Opera* were expressed but support came from the Earl of Carlisle. He was alarmed by the growth of Methodism in Manchester, and stated that he knew no more effectual way 'to eradicate that dark, odious, and ridiculous enthusiasm as by giving to the people cheerful, rational amusements, which may operate against their methodistical melancholy'.[1]

The grant, dated July 3, 1775, was made to Joseph Younger and George Mattocks, their executors, administrators and assigns, for the term of twenty-one years from June 15. The stated terms were 'to establish a Theatre in Manchester, to keep a company of comedians for His Majesty's Service, and to act such Tragedies, Plays, Operas, and Entertainments only as had been or should be licensed by the Lord Chamberlain of His Majesty's Household'.

A sum of £2000 was raised, forty subscribers each contributing £50,[2] and the building was erected on land pur-

75

chased from Thomas Caygill Worsley at the junction of York Street and Spring Gardens on the site now occupied by the Westminster Bank. The structure was of brick, without any external decoration, and measured approximately 102 feet by 48 feet.[3]

At this date Manchester was growing in population, but a survey made by Rev. John Whitaker in 1773 gave a total of no more than 27,246, including Salford. Richard Arkwright's patent for spinning by means of rollers was granted in 1769 and the improvements by Samuel Crompton appeared in 1779. These and other inventions were rapidly to transform Manchester from a country town to a vast centre of industry, but in 1775 the process had only just begun. Deansgate on the one side and Mosley Street on the other virtually bounded the populous area, and Market Street Lane,[4] with its black-and-white houses without any pretence of a consistent building line, remained little changed from Stuart times, though it was the main artery of the town. In it, when the first Manchester directory was issued in 1772,[5] lived eighty-five families, representing forty-three occupations, which included two surgeons, tea dealers and bankers, a boarding school for young ladies, and some now unfamiliar tradesmen such as a snag-maker and a pattern-maker. Several fine residences, notably that of Mr. Dickenson where the Young Pretender had stayed in 1745, were also in the street, and ten inns are named. In the area where Victoria Station now stands were large residences with good gardens and what is now London Road Station was open fields. By an Act of 1708 St. Ann's Church and Square were erected, it being stipulated that the square should be thirty yards wide to enable the statutory Acres Fair to be held there as before. St. Ann's Square had become, by the mid-eighteenth century, one of the main residential areas, but the Fair continued to be held there until 1821. The first step towards improving

street conditions was taken in the year the Theatre Royal
was erected, but Market Street Lane remained much as it
was to the end of the century. In fact the little River Tib,
approaching alongside a footpath shaded by trees from what
is now Oldham Road, ran its uninhibited course down
Market Street Lane until covered over in 1783.

Joseph Harrop,[6] the proprietor of the *Manchester Mercury*,
appears to have been the direct lessee of the theatre from the
subscribers; it was he who acted in business affairs and was
responsible for the rebuilding after fire in 1790. This may
account for the interest taken by his paper in the affairs of
the theatre. Harrop certainly made a success of his newspaper, and his enterprise is shown by his scheme to send to
Derby to pick up the London news and get it back to Manchester and printed before the London papers arrived.

Of the two patentees, Younger had for a time been
prompter at Covent Garden as well as appearing at most
provincial theatres. If Tate Wilkinson is to be taken seriously,
his abilities as actor were not great. He was a corpulent man,
and Wilkinson recounts amusing anecdotes which turn on
his size and his passion for playing unsuitable parts. For
Younger as a man, however, Wilkinson has nothing but
praise. He speaks of his 'true honesty, worth and good principles', and continues: 'Younger was remarkable for being
firm in his attachment to any gentleman, lady or dependent,
or any person whatever, whom he wished well or that he
judged worthy his support, and he has, I believe, often hurt
himself to serve others'.[7] Mattocks, who had built some
reputation at Covent Garden as a singer, was a man of style
and fashion. John Bernard tells of the impression he received
as a small boy of Mattocks at Portsmouth, 'arrayed in a gold-
laced suit of green and white, with a bag-wig, three-cornered
cocked hat, a silver-mounted cane, and a silver-handled
hanger', with his 'swan-like dignity' and 'stand-out-of-the-

way consequence'. As an acting vocalist Bernard thought only Vernon his superior.[8]

Younger and Mattocks also controlled the Liverpool theatre, where the season ran from about June to October. In theory, at least, the company there was drawn from actors of the London theatres during the off season, and Liverpool was so jealous of this distinction that various disturbances arose when they suspected that actors not blessed by London approval were being introduced to them. The result of this Liverpool policy was that, although Manchester's season did not overlap that of Liverpool, the company was by no means the same at both houses, particularly in the early years. In practice, of course, most of the actors did not have London engagements and moved between the two cities. But the Liverpool policy accounts for the fact that Mr. and Mrs. Mattocks, for instance, were rarely seen at Manchester in the early years. From the season of 1786–87 Manchester and Liverpool operated separately, and for some years thereafter the Manchester season lasted seven or eight months, and for the rest of the year the players took what engagements they could find elsewhere. Wilkinson used this as an argument to show that he, by giving full-time engagements, held a great advantage. In the middle nineties this difference was removed, when Manchester became the main centre of a circuit which included Chester, Shrewsbury and Lichfield and was in action throughout most of the year.

During the greater part of our period the Manchester theatre was open on Monday, Wednesday and Friday each week. There were slight deviations, such as the substitution of Shrove Tuesday for Ash Wednesday and alterations at Christmas and Easter. During Whit-week, which was also Race Week, plays were normally performed each night, and in some years seasons were arranged to coincide with the musical festival in September. In many years also, special engagements were played during the closed season, the supporting company being gathered together for the occasion. Towards the end of our period Thursday was often added as an extra playing night.[9]

The normal prices of admission were three shillings for places in the boxes, two shillings in the pit and one shilling in the gallery. The practice, prevalent in the period, of allowing patrons to enter for half-price after the main piece, seems never to have been followed in Manchester. Subscribers, as shareholders in the theatre were called, received permanent tickets entitling them to attend all performances, and these were not only transferable for a single occasion, but apparently could be sold for the season, as is clear from an advertisement in the *Mercury* of November 21, 1786, when W. Stevenson was willing 'to dispose of one, two or three Perpetual Tickets for the Theatre Royal the next season'. In some years, as will be seen, the managers offered season tickets, but this does not appear to have been the general practice. It was always possible to book seats (or "places") in the boxes in advance, and for the rest of the house to obtain beforehand tickets which did not guarantee a seat. These were copper tickets, usually called checks, and they were collected at boxes distinct from the box-office as the patrons entered the theatre.

Very important for the actors was the benefit system. Several weeks towards the end of each season were taken up with benefits; members of the orchestra, the front of the house staff and the lesser fry among the players had to share, sometimes with many others, sometimes with one other, but the main players enjoyed a sole benefit. They were responsible for the charges of the performance and had also to pay the managers a 'house charge'. For the rest, the night's receipts were their own. It was an unsatisfactory system, but prevailed everywhere at this time. The advantage lay clearly with the managers, who could offer lower salaries with the promise of a benefit; who were protected from loss by the house charge; and who were given a hold over their players, since anything would be suffered rather than depart without the benefit money. For the actors it could be either a blessing or a liability. They were at the mercy of public opinion and of hazards such as bad weather. They went to great lengths to tempt audiences to their support, and the system undoubtedly added to the almost abject servility which marked the players' attitude to the public. A popular actor might do well, but woe betide one who had incurred censure, however unwarranted. Some actors succeeded in enlisting aid; the Freemasons or the military would often act as patrons, or more occasionally, individuals of social importance. It is only fair to add that some managers acted generously. Actors were given special benefits for personal misfortunes, or were granted a second when the first one failed; and benefits were often granted, not only for charity, but to persons who seemed to have no real claim to them.[10]

A manuscript in the British Museum,[11] in the form of instructions from Younger to the Treasurer, William Barry, for the regulation of the Liverpool and Manchester theatres, supplies many interesting details, and since such documents for the provincial theatres are all too rare, it is worth quoting at some length. It is, unfortunately, only a draft, and many tantalising blanks are left. There is no date, but as it relates to both theatres, and Barry died in 1780, it must be within the period 1775–80. In fact, from internal evidence, it can be dated with some confidence as belonging to the season 1777–78.[12]

After instructing Barry to make weekly deductions from the salaries of certain actors until their debts are satisfied, Younger goes on to detail the procedure in the house for dealing with checks and money:

Mr. Barry is to return the Account of his numbering sealed up to Mr. Younger or in his absence to Mr. Powell every night before he takes the Office Keepers Account—The Money is to be put into one box and the Checks into another and if any Person wants their money again before the Curtain is drawn up—the Check Taker is to deliver them a Card of which each Check Taker is to have twenty on a night and on their giving this Card to the Office Keeper he is to return their Money and the Card to tell as Cost for him against the Checks in the settling of his Accounts. Every Office Keeper to be furnished with Silver to the Value of [blank] each night to give change with. If any Check Taker is found to let any Person pass him without delivering his Check which he is to put directly into the Box—or if he receives anything but checks—or is found delaying the putting them in the Box he will be discharged directly. A written Notice viz—No Money is taken at this Hatch or anything admitted but Copper Tickets—to be stuck up at the Place of each Check Taker. The Money Boxes and Accounts to be sent every night to Mr. Barry—the Check Boxes to Mr. Younger when there when he is absent to Mr. Powell. The Office Keeper to have his remaining Checks counted every night if any missing to pay the Value of Admission for each. The Check Taker to do the same by his Cards which he is to send with the Check Boxes to Mr. Younger or in his absence to Mr. Powell. Mr. Younger or Mr. Powell and Mr. Barry to settle the Account of the House every morning after the Rehearsal of the Play—Doorkeepers Accts to be sent for at difft time.

The importance of candles in the economics of eighteenth century theatres is indicated by the next batch of instructions:

The Number of Candles wanted for the Stage and Dressing Rooms to be ascertained and delivered out every night by Mr. Barry and in the morning as many Peices returned to the Cellar in his Presence—once a month they are to be recounted and returned to the Chandler and the Value allowed against his Acct.

The oil was to be measured and delivered in Mr. Barry's presence every morning and 'no Person but himself is to have the Key of the Cellar'. The number and maximum cost of playbills is dealt with, but unfortunately blanks occur here in the manuscript and the only price inserted is of one shilling per hundred for printing the small bills.

Mr. Barry's duties by no means ended there. 'No Servants or Hairdressers to be admitted behind the Scenes after the Curtain is up belong to whom they will' and it was Barry's duty to see that the house was cleared of them 'during the playing of the last Musick—and the chairwomen are to attend in the Hall for the purpose of carrying in any of the Performers things'. No chorus singers were to be employed 'or more Extras than cannot be avoided—the Bill for them to be signed by the Prompter and they are to be paid by Mr. Barry the morning after the play, and the numbers used put upon the back of his Account'.

Barry's final duties were to make a set of Manchester books for Mattocks, and to keep all his accounts regularly entered every week. 'These must be done out of hand and on no pretence neglected in future'. No doubt the final words provide the clue for the whole memorandum.

The first performance in the new theatre was on Whit-Monday, June 5, 1775, when the programme included *Othello*. Younger played Othello; Casey, Iago; Mrs. Ward, Desdemona; and Mrs. Kniveton, Emilia. There does not appear to be any evidence to support Broadbent's statement that the building was at this date uncompleted.[13] It could be so, but it is not necessary to make the assumption to account for the break between Whit and October. The managers used their Liverpool company to take advantage of the Manchester holiday week, but were committed to return to Liverpool. Whitweek at no time formed part of the normal Manchester season.

On October 3 the *Mercury* announced that the winter season would start on October 9. We do not know the opening programme, but on October 11 were performed *The Fair Penitent* and *Thomas and Sally*. Since this was the start of a new theatre, it may be of interest to give the full company: Younger, Ward, Casey, Lane, Weston, Wood, Collins, Bates, Connor, Gloster, Barnshaw, Hollingsworth, Herryman, Kennedy, Cawdell, Powell, Cummins, Mrs. Farren and her three daughters, Elizabeth, Margaret and Kitty, Mrs. Ward, Mrs. Kniveton, Mrs. Taplin, Mrs. Hartley, Mrs. Hart, Mrs. Thompson, Miss Singleton, Miss Potir, Miss Atkinson. For most of our period the company was of about this size—a minimum of thirty and a maximum of thirty-five.

The leading parts during this first season were well distributed. Younger appeared as Macbeth, Prospero and King John; Collins as Othello and Shylock; Ward as Romeo, Bassanio and Orlando; Powell as Henry V; Casey as Iago and Jaques; and Cawdell as Lord Townley. Among the women Mrs. Ward had a large share of leading parts, but Mrs. Taplin played Lady Townley, Rosalind, and Lydia Languish. For December 20 *The Tempest* (as altered from Shakespeare by Dryden) was performed with 'The Music, Dresses, Scenes, Machinery, Showers of Fire, Storm, Ship Wreck, and every other Decoration proper to the Play entirely new'. This was the version in which Miranda is provided with a sister, Dorinda, and the parts were played by Mrs. Kniveton and Elizabeth Farren. There was also promised a 'Grand Dance of Furies', the whole to conclude 'with a view of the calm sea and a Grand Masque between Neptune and Amphitrite in a Chariot drawn by Sea Horses surrounded by Tritons etc.' This performance was repeated six days later as the Boxing Day attraction. The only visiting novelty during this season was Signor Firzi and his Pupils, who promised 'several new and surprising feats'.

Before the second season started Younger indulged in

several weeks advance publicity for his special engagement of Signor Rossignoll, who would imitate many kinds of birds 'with the voice only' and would also 'lead a Band of Music on a Fiddle without Strings, in a Concerto of his own composing'. Younger also assured his public that 'Every piece produced at Drury Lane and Covent Garden this Winter that can be done out of London will be prepared with all expedition'.

It is neither Signor Rossignoll nor the plays performed that make this season probably, in retrospect, the most interesting in Manchester's theatre history, but the coming of Mrs. Siddons, Mrs. Inchbald and John Philip Kemble. Although Mrs. Siddons was not yet twenty-two, she had already experienced the hopes and then the disappointment of a London engagement. Only six months before, on June 5, 1776, she had ended a season at Drury Lane, a season which also marked the end of Garrick's long career, and she was at Birmingham when the news reached her that she would not be re-engaged. The seasons in Manchester began that seven years' climb back which was to establish her as the greatest actress of her day.

Mrs. Inchbald, who had met Mrs. Siddons in Liverpool and begun a friendship that was to last throughout their lives, was not a great actress, but she was a beautiful and talented woman who won fame as a dramatist and novelist, and became one of the best known and most highly respected figures of the period. When we remember that Elizabeth Farren was also at Manchester, we may well wonder whether any provincial stock company ever included at the same time three more remarkable women.

Mrs. Siddons, 'of the Theatre Royal, Drury Lane', made her debut in Manchester on December 18, 1776, as Mrs. Montague in *A Word to the Wise*. Two nights later Mrs. Inchbald, 'from Edinburgh', appeared as Jane Shore in

Rowe's tragedy of that name. On Boxing Day she was Lady
Percy in *Henry IV, Part I,* her husband playing Westmor-
land and Siddons playing Douglas. The Falstaff was Ward;
the King was Younger. For New Year's Day there was a
production of *The Royal Martyr* in which Mrs. Siddons
played Lady Fairfax and Mrs. Inchbald was the Queen. The
play was dressed 'in the Habits of the Times' and in Act IV
would be introduced 'the Grand Scene of the Trial of the
King, with a representation of the Scaffolding which was
erected for the Reception of Peers, Peeresses, Ambassadors,
etc., at the State Trial of her Grace the Duchess of Kingston'.
After the play was promised a 'Comic Dance call'd The
Wapping Landlady, or Jack in Distress, in which will be
introduced the Scene of the Ship Wreck from "The Tempest" '. This, in turn, was followed by 'The Grand Representation of the Regatta, with the Rowing of Boats for the
Coat and Badge, as performed several nights last Winter at
Drury Lane'. Nor was this all, for the evening ended with
the farce *Miss in Her Teens.* It is hardly surprising that the
performance started at six instead of the usual seven.

The Royal Martyr was repeated on January 8, and a week
later Mrs. Siddons played Mistress Page to the Page of her
husband, the Falstaff of Ward, the Ford of Younger and the
Shallow of Inchbald.

Connor received a benefit on January 20 and chose Con-
greve's *Love for Love,* which was given the sub-title *The
Humours of Ben the Sailor.* It had been 'pruned of all the
Indelicacies which have formerly rendered it exceptionable'.
Mrs. Siddons played Angelica to the Valentine of Powell,
and Connor was Ben (with a song). Rich's famous panto-
mime *Harlequin Dr. Faustus,* reached its seventh perform-
ance of the season on January 21, when the main piece was
Dryden's *All for Love* with Mrs. Inchbald as Cleopatra and
Mrs. Siddons as Dollabella. The Antony was Powell. Casey

announced at his benefit on January 24 that he would quit the stage at the end of the season.

It was on Wednesday, January 29, that John Philip Kemble made his first appearance. He was only nineteen, but since leaving school at Douay and flouting his father's hopes by becoming an actor, he had first appeared at Wolverhampton almost exactly twelve months before going to Manchester and thereafter seems to have had varied experiences but little success. If, as was usual, he was given the power to choose his own part for a first appearance with the company, he was evidently, at that early date, in no danger of underestimating his powers, for his choice was Othello. His sister was Desdemona, and Younger played Iago.

Two days prior to this Mrs. Siddons had appeared as Semiramis in Ayscough's tragedy of that name, first produced at Drury Lane a month earlier, and she repeated the performance for Miss Farren's benefit on February 3. The *Mercury,* which so far had been strangely silent on the affairs of the theatre, informs us that 'the Epilogue has been allowed by the first People of Literature to be one of the First Productions, for firm Sentiment and fine Poetry—it was exceedingly well delivered by Mrs. Siddons'. For this piece we are also given comments on the scenery: 'the two scenes painted purposely for this play by Mr. Hodgings are truly Elegant and Picturesque; the outside of the Palace of Semiramis, with the Hanging Gardens on one hand and the Mausoleums on the other, are allowed to be very near representations of the descriptions given by Historians'. After the main piece at Miss Farren's benefit there was a performance of *Cymon* in which she played Fatima (with a song) Siddons was Cymon and Mrs. Siddons Sylvia. Hodgings had evidently been busy on this also, for patrons were promised 'a view of the Burning Lake, the Flying Chariot drawn by Eagles, Inchanted black Tower, Transparent Cave of Mer-

lin, etc'. There was also to be a 'Procession of the Knights of
the Order of Chivalry' and an original epilogue spoken by
Miss Farren.

For Barnshaw's benefit Kemble was Young Norval and
Mrs. Siddons Lady Randolph in *Douglas* and when *The
Merchant of Venice* (incidentally described as a tragedy)
was revived on February 7 Mrs. Siddons was Portia to the
Shylock of Younger. The parts of Lorenzo and Jessica (both
provided with songs) were played by Siddons and Miss
Farren.

The dancers engaged this season were a brother and sister,
Mr. and Miss West, 'who were trained by the celebrated
Signor Grimaldi' and for their benefits they each announced
an enormous programme. West began with *False Delicacy*
in which Mrs. Inchbald, Miss Farren and Mrs. Siddons
appeared as Lady Betty, Miss Marchmont and Mrs. Hartley.
At the end of each act the Wests had their fling. After Act I
there was a comic dance, 'The Cowkeepers'; after Act II a
grand ballad dance, 'The Medley'; after Act III, 'for this
night only', a 'new grand Pastoral Ballad Dance, Middleton
Wake or the Milkmaids Maypole' to be performed by 'Forty
Children of the Town, all to be dressed in new Dresses for
that Purpose; as it was performed at the Theatre Royal,
Drury Lane, twenty-three nights successively' (for Miss
West's benefit this had become 'Eccles Wake, with the
Humours of Pendleton Posey') and after Act IV a new Pantomime Dance, 'Mercury Harlequin in Manchester', during
which Miss West promised to jump five feet high. To round
off the evening, West (his fifth attempt as actor on any
stage) played Abel Drugger in *The Tobacconist,* an adaptation from Ben Jonson. The programme for Miss West's
benefit followed a similar pattern, save that one dance had
been performed 'by Mr. and Miss West before their Majesties and the Royal Family at their Palace at Kew, and

repeated twice in the same evening by Command of their Majesties'.

Powell played *Coriolanus,* announced as 'never acted here', for his benefit, with Mrs. Siddons as Veturia, and at a joint benefit for the Inchbalds *All in the Wrong* was given with Powell as Belmont, Inchbald as Sir John Restless, Mrs. Inchbald as Belinda and Mrs. Siddons as Lady Restless.

The announcement of *The Clandestine Marriage* for the joint benefit of Lane and Jefferson (prompter) was accompanied by a statement that 'Mrs. Siddons being too ill to perform so trying a character as the Grecian Daughter, Mr. Lane and Mr. Jefferson are under the Necessity of changing to the above Play'. Two days later, however, Mrs. Siddons played Cleone to her brother's Glanville for Cawdell's benefit, and on February 24 she appeared for her benefit in what was to become one of her greatest parts, Queen Catherine in *Henry VIII.* Inchbald was Henry, Younger played Wolsey and Mrs. Inchbald Anne Bullen. As seems to have been the custom at this period, Bishop Gardiner was played by a low comedian, Connor.

Hodgings's scene paintings called for special mention when *King Arthur* was given, 'with the original music by Purcell'. His scenes consisted of 'a very fine wintry view of Frost and Snow, which changes to an extensive Summer Prospect of a Garden, etc., the Bleeding Tree, the Golden Bridge at which two Syrens or Mermaids appear and sing their deluding strains'.

Kemble, whose opportunities had been strictly limited, shared a benefit with his brother-in-law on March 19, and Mrs. Siddons performed Hamlet ('being her second appearance in that character'). She was supported by Inchbald (Claudius), Siddons (Horatio), Kemble (Laertes), Connor (Polonius), Miss Farren (Ophelia), Mrs. Inchbald (Gertrude) and Younger as what must have been a very substantial Ghost. This appears to have been Garrick's version, which omitted the Gravediggers. Incredible as it may seem to us now, there were comic dances between the acts, and at the close a song "Written on a Manufacturing Town" by G. A. Stevens and sung by Siddons. The season ended two nights later, when Mrs. Siddons played Mrs. Oakly to the Oakly of Younger in a performance of *The Jealous Wife* for the manager's benefit.

We would give much for details of these performances in Mrs. Siddons's first season in Manchester, but we do not even know all the parts she performed, as Monday's programme was seldom advertised in the *Mercury*. It is possible to add the following to those already given: Indiana (*The Conscious Lovers*), Clarissa (*The Hotel*), Lady Sadlife (*The Double Gallant*), Andromache (*The Distrest Mother*), Countess of Somerset (*Sir Thomas Overbury*), Mandane (*Cyrus*) and The First Spirit (*The Installation*). Among Kemble's other parts were Castalia (*The Orphan*) and Orestes (*The Distrest Mother*).

During Race Week Mrs. Siddons played Mrs. Sullen in *The Beaux Stratagem* and there was an announcement that 'Miss Farren of our Theatre is engaged by Mr. Colman to perform this Summer at the Theatre Royal in the Haymarket but has obtained leave of Absence for this week that the Performances intended for the Races may not meet with any Disappointments'. Before leaving this season it may be worth mentioning that the company had included Mr. and Mrs. Stanfield, the parents of Clarkson Stanfield, who won fame as a painter both inside and outside the theatre.

Between the regular season and Race Week Mr. and Mrs. Siddons fulfilled a short engagement with Tate Wilkinson, and his comments make up for the lack of material about her Manchester season. She was, he tells us, 'the leader of theatrical fashion in Manchester', and although rejected in

London, 'that truly intrinsic merit, that unquenchable flame of soul and spirit, prevented even London prejudice to hurt her in the opinion of country audiences', He was concerned about her health, but that was the only doubt. 'I never remember so great a favourite, as a York actress, as Mrs. Siddons was in that short period—every one lifted their eyes with astonishment, that such a face, judgment, etc., could have been neglected by the London audience, and by the first actor of the world (Mr. Garrick) as if not of sterling worth'. Wilkinson hoped to persuade her to remain, and admits that he tempted her with a wardrobe better than anything Younger could offer, but she refused him.[14]

On September 17, 18, and 19, 1777, a Festival of Music (said to have been the first of its kind in England) was held at Manchester, and to coincide with it Younger and Mattocks arranged a short season in which both Mr. and Mrs. Mattocks appeared, their duties at Covent Garden having ended for the summer. Beginning on Monday, September 15, there were performances each night that week except Thursday, there being a concert on that night (the other festival performances were held in the morning). Mrs. Mattocks played the Maid to her husband's Lord Aimworth in *The Maid of the Mill;* The Countess of Salisbury, in the play of that name, to Kemble's Alwin, and for her benefit *Know Your Own Mind,* it being stated that, although the play was not yet printed, the manuscript had been loaned to her for that night only. Mrs. Mattocks had first appeared as a child in 1753 and her long and varied career lasted until 1808. As a singer she obtained fame outside the theatre and in 1769 she was a principal vocalist at the Three Choirs Festival at Gloucester.[15]

The Theatre Royal programmes contained a high percentage of musical pieces, ranging from ballad operas to musical farces and interludes. In a large number of non-musical pieces, songs and dances were introduced, and these ranged from the songs sung by Jessica and Lorenzo in *The Merchant of Venice* to those of Widow Brady in *The Irish Widow* and the many songs incorporated in plays or sung between the acts by comedians such as Munden, Cherry, Barrett and Ryley. The company always possessed one of each sex engaged specially as vocalists—Tannett, Wood, Bellamy, T. Smith, Mrs. Peile, Mrs. Addison, and Miss Griffiths, for example—but the conditions of stock company playing required not only that these should appear in non-musical parts, but that the majority of the company should be able to take a share in musical pieces. That Manchester was noted for its musical pieces is indicated by many references, from those by the German, Küttner (whose views on the theatre generally appear later in this book) to those by the writers in the *Monthly Mirror* at the end of our period.

In this period, too, the relation between the theatre and the musical world outside was close. The theatre orchestra (usually called the band) always contained one or more instrumentalists who were also church organists, and a great amount of music was written for the theatre by these men and also by other church organists who were not employed at the theatre. Wainwright, Buckley, Cheese, Barber and Haigh may be mentioned in this connection. For instrumentalists in Manchester there was no lack of employment. Many members of the theatre orchestra played also at the Circus; in oratorios and festivals as far afield as Preston, Chester, Blackpool and Halifax, as well as in Manchester and surrounding districts; on occasions such as the Chester and Knutsford Races; and in the many Assemblies and Promenades scattered throughout the year. Many artistes engaged for the musical festivals appeared also in musical pieces at the theatre during their visits, and the theatre was used frequently for concerts by local or visiting musicians.

Manchester was always a musical city. The Gentlemen's Concert Club, which sponsored the festivals, was founded in 1770, and in 1775, the year of the opening of the Theatre Royal, the foundation stone of their Concert Room in Fountain Street was laid. There were also musical societies in Oldham, Ashton-under-Lyne and other neighbouring towns, and the pages of the *Mercury* testify to intense musical activity.

The Inchbalds were missing from the company which started a new season on December 19, 1777, and the Wards, the Stanfields, Cawdell, Lane, Casey and Jefferson had also gone. To fill the gaps came Lee Lewes, whose *Memoirs* have supplied much information (and misinformation) on the theatre of that period; Vincent, who later became a clergyman and schoolmaster, and who occupies several pages of *The Wandering Patentee*;[16] Townshend, Platt and Phillips. Hollingsworth, over the years one of the most popular of low comedians in Liverpool and Manchester, returned; the newcomers among the ladies were Mrs. Symons, Miss Dillon, Mrs. Watson, and Miss Evans. The last-named lady married Powell before the season was a month old.

The Merry Wives of Windsor started the season, with Mrs. Siddons again as Mistress Page, Mrs. Kniveton as Mistress Ford and Lewes as Falstaff. The Caius was Floor, whose main duty was as prompter in place of Jefferson. He merits mention here as he is said to have recommended Mrs. Siddons to the Bath manager. On Boxing Day the main piece was *Merope,* in which Vincent made his first appearance as Dorilas to the Merope of Mrs. Siddons and the Poliphontes of Kemble. *Romeo and Juliet* followed on December 30 with Vincent and Mrs. Siddons in the title parts and Mrs. Symons as the Nurse.

It had been announced earlier that Miss Farren, whilst in London, had been taking singing lessons from Battishill, and had played the part of Rosetta in *Love in a Village* at the Haymarket. She repeated the part in Manchester, and appeared during the season in several other musical pieces, the company being less well endowed with singers than usual. The Edinburgh manager, West Digges, played a special engagement, one of his parts being Falstaff in *Henry IV* in which Kemble was Hotspur. On the same night Mrs. Siddons made one of her rare appearances in farce, as Widow Brady in *The Irish Widow,* 'with the original song'.

The pantomime, *Harlequin Dr. Faustus,* the performances of which had reached double figures in the previous season, started again triumphantly, adding new scenes as it went, but soon it gave way to *The Birth and Adventures of Harlequin,* which was constantly revived during the season. This piece introduced two local scenes, 'The Canal or Cut belonging to his Grace the Duke of Bridgwater at Barton Bridge' and 'The Village of Eccles'.

When playing Sigismunda in *Tancred and Sigismunda* on January 10, reported the *Mercury,* 'Mrs. Siddons was taken so extremely ill, that it was with great difficulty she finished the character'. As a result, a production of *Percy* was postponed, and it was doubtless for the same reason that Miss Farren made her 'first capital attempt in tragedy' by playing Cordelia to the Lear of John Lee during that actor's first visit to Manchester since the Marsden Street days.

Mrs. Siddons was back on the stage by February 18, when she played Mrs. Neville in *Know Your Own Mind* to the Millamour of Kemble. For her benefit a month later she chose Isabella in the play of that name, a part which was to become inseparably associated with her. The afterpiece was *The Devil to Pay,* in which 'for that night only' she was seen as Nell 'with all the songs'. The advertisement for this night contained the following note: 'Least a Report (already propagated) should gain ground, that all the Boxes are taken for this Night, Mrs. Siddons begs leave to assure the Public at the Time this Advertisement went to Press, there was a full half disengaged'.

Kemble's benefit began with *Edward the Black Prince,* with Kemble in the title part and his sister as Mariana. It was followed 'for this night only' by a piece he had written called *The Female Officer, or Royal Volunteer,* in which Mrs. Siddons appeared. There was also an ode, "The Praises of Manchester", written by 'A Gentleman of the Town and delivered in the Character of Liberty by Mr. Kemble'.

In addition to the parts already mentioned and those revived from the previous season, Mrs. Siddons appeared as Portia (*Julius Caesar*), Elwina (*Percy*), Jocasta (*Codrus*), Euphrasia (*The Grecian Daughter*), Palmira (*Mahomet*), and Fair Rosamond (*Henry II*). Kemble advanced in importance, playing Mahomet, Codrus, Dionysius (*The Grecian Daughter*), Earl Douglas (*Percy*), Darnley (*The Hypocrite*), and Cassius, in addition to those previously named.

The great event of Race Week was Manchester's first hearing of *The School for Scandal,* which had been produced at Drury Lane rather more than a year previously. It was still unprinted, but Younger announced that a copy had been given to him 'by Mr. Sheridan, with permission to play'. The Manchester performance was on June 9, the main cast being: Bates (Sir Peter Teazle), Younger (Sir Oliver), Kemble (Joseph Surface), Lewes (Charles Surface), Siddons (Sir Benjamin), Powell (Moses), Hollingsworth (Rowley), Mrs. Siddons (Lady Teazle), Mrs. Kniveton (Mrs. Candour), Mrs. Watson (Lady Sneerwell), and Miss Dillon (Maria).

Mr. and Mrs. Siddons, Kemble and the Farren family (the youngest daughter, Kitty, had died the previous year) now ended their careers as stock players in Manchester, and the company which assembled for the start of a new season on November 4, 1778, showed many changes. Mr. and Mrs. Ward returned, and the newcomers included Tannett, who played singing parts and was announced as 'a pupil of Hooke, a gentleman famous in the musical world'; Follett, 'several years comedian at Drury Lane and Richmond'; Miss Sharpe, who had appeared a few times at Drury Lane during Garrick's last season; Gardner, R. Palmer, and Mrs. Hunter, who joined the company some weeks after the start. Younger had also engaged the dancers, Mr. and Miss West, to appear for twelve nights.

At the opening performance Miss Sharpe played Rosetta in *Love in a Village* to the Meadows of Tannett. As might be expected the Wests contrived some notable fare for their benefits. For West *The Rivals* was given on November 27 with Powell as Captain Absolute and the Wards as Faulkland and Julia. After the first act a 'new comic dance' was introduced, called 'The Humours of Kersal Moor Races', announced to conclude 'with a match between Sir Harry Crofts (West) and Lord Jostle (Bates) who will Ride their own Ponies'. A postscript assured the audience that 'the Stage will be posted and corded round in the Form of the Course'. Bates, whose nickname was 'Harlequin', was usually called upon when pantomimic clowning was needed. West continued his programme with a new pantomime, *Oriental Magick,* during which Miss West promised to improve on her previous feat by jumping six feet high. To conclude there was a pastoral dance, 'Rural Grace', in which sixty local children appeared.

Hamlet was performed twice during the season. Ward (Hamlet), Gardner (Claudius), Connor (Polonius), Miss Sharpe (Ophelia), and Younger (Ghost), were in the cast both times, but the Gertrude was first Mrs. Ward and then Mrs. Hunter. The gravediggers were restored and played by

Powell and Hollingsworth. The new pantomime, *Oriental Magick*, was evidently as popular as its predecessors and was repeated many times.

Sheridan's 'Musical Entertainment' called *The Camp* seems to have been one of the successes of the season. One of its scenes was 'A Picturesque view of the Camp of last Summer at Coxheath' and the *Mercury* announced that 'it was, by particular permission of the Managers (of Drury Lane) painted in London by Mr. Hodgings, from the Original Scene designed by Mons. Loutenbourgh'.[17] After expressing satisfaction at the whole production, the *Mercury* continued, 'it would be great injustice not to particularize Miss Sharpe's adroitness in the Management of her Firelock'. She had played the part of Nancy, 'a young recruit'. *The Camp* received several performances.

Mrs. Hunter was the Lady Teazle in a revival of *The School for Scandal* and Mrs. Smith, another of the newcomers that season, played Imogen to the Posthumus of Ward in *Cymbeline*. During Race Week Mrs. Mattocks played a round of characters, including Lady Teazle.

There was a late start to the next season, no performance being given until January 5, 1780. In the meantime Miss Sharpe had married Robert Palmer, one of three actor brothers, of whom only one, John, obtained any notable success. The Palmers were both there for the new season, and the only newcomer of interest was Robertson. Broadbent is in no doubt that this is James Shaftoe Robertson, the founder of a famous theatrical family which was to produce T. W. Robertson and Mrs. Kendal. There was at this period another James Robertson playing in provincial theatres and there is no real evidence which of them was at Manchester.

An early event was the first Manchester production of Sheridan's *The Duenna* 'by permission of the author, from the original copy'. The cast included Tannett, Brett and

Mrs. Palmer. For the first time since the Marsden Street days, Massinger's *A New Way to Pay Old Debts* was performed, and when Mrs. Ward took her benefit she chose *The Winter's Tale* and ended the evening with an 'Address to the Ladies and Gentlemen of Manchester in the character of Britannia'. Looking back, it seems odd that Mrs. Siddons had been given no opportunity to play Lady Macbeth in Manchester, but the revival this season was the first for four years. Younger and Mrs. Ward took the leading parts. Younger then announced in the *Mercury* that:

> he ventures (for the first time) to attempt the part of Falstaff, and as he is conscious how very difficult a task he has undertaken he hopes for that indulgence he has so continually experienced in Manchester. His motive for this attempt is, that from the great difficulty there is to procure a performer suitable to this character, three of Shakespeare's best plays are obliged to be laid aside. If he is so lucky as to succeed, it will be the means of keeping them on at this Theatre; but if he should not be fortunate enough to please the publick, he will not attempt to obtrude himself a second time in this piece.

The performance of *Henry IV* was on March 8. As Younger played Falstaff frequently after this, it must be assumed that he satisfied his public.

At Easter there was a new pantomime, *The Lancashire Witches*, for which the music was composed by Richard Wainwright, at that time organist at St. Ann's Church. Banks painted the scenery, which depicted the Dock Gates at Liverpool, and various Manchester scenes including The Exchange, the Bull's Head, the Infirmary, and 'a new rural scene, representing Ardwick Green'. On April 17 Younger was able to announce another new piece for Mrs. Kniveton's benefit, 'Mr. Sheridan having been so indulgent as to favour Mr. Younger with his celebrated entertainment of "The Critic", which has been performed upwards of thirty nights this season at the Theatre Royal, Drury Lane'. It was further announced that 'the model of the scenery has been copied by Mr. Hodgings from that used at Drury Lane, painted under the direction of Monsieur de Loutherbourg, and will be executed here by Mr. Banks'. The cast at Manchester included Ward (Puff), Robertson (Plagiary), Hollingsworth (Dangle), Mrs. Kniveton (Tilburnia), and Mrs. Tannett (Confidant).

William Barry, the treasurer, had died (he was a brother of Spranger Barry) and in the *Mercury* for May 2, 1780, a notice appeared: 'Mr. Younger having appointed Friday, May 12th, for the use of the creditors of the late Mr. Barry, they are requested to take notice, that they may be furnished with tickets to the amount of their respective debts, free from all deduction or demand whatever, by sending on Tuesday week to Mr. Barnes, at his office at the Theatre'. On the appointed night the manager again appeared as Falstaff, and in the *Mercury* of May 16 a further notice stated that, as a result of the performance, '£92 of his debts are paid out of the sum of £117, which the demands sent in amounted to'.

Younger, during Race Week, continued to leave his public in no doubt of the efforts he was making on their behalf by performing *The Belle's Stratagem*, of which 'he has with great difficulty procured a copy' and then 'under such restrictions that it can only be performed here once'.

For the next season the chief newcomer was Mrs. Massey. On January 17, 1781, Manchester for the first time saw *The Comedy of Errors*, 'written by Shakespeare and altered by Mr. Hull'. There was some little trouble before Robertson enjoyed his benefit. In a long announcement he stated that an anonymous letter had been received, informing him that if he went forward with his plans to perform *Elmira,* which had been licensed for the occasion, 'his interests will suffer very materially in the Boxes'. He bowed to the public's request and would play *The Clandestine Marriage* instead. Although during the rest of the season Younger continued to introduce plays recently given in London, there was nothing of particular note. For Race Week, William Farren (not related to the family of Elizabeth Farren) appeared as Othello.

This proved to be the last full season under Younger's control. For the special season in September to entertain the public assembled for the Musical Festival, he let the theatre to a company controlled by Austin and Whitlock, and when the time came round for the regular winter season the same pair took over, possibly owing to the failing health of Younger.

II

1781—1789

THE COMPANY owned by Austin[18] and Whitlock had an extensive circuit, which included Chester, Newcastle-on-Tyne, Preston, Lancaster and Whitehaven and, according to Winston, involved them in travelling eleven hundred miles each year.[19] Joseph Austin had played at Drury Lane under Garrick from 1758 to 1761, and by 1766 he was joint owner with Heatton of a strolling company. Heatton retired in favour of Charles Edward Whitlock, said to be a native of Manchester and a godson of the Young Pretender.[20] Whitlock later (in 1785) married Elizabeth Kemble, a sister of Mrs. Siddons, and they remained associated with this company until going to America in 1793.

As this was a settled company playing throughout the year,[21] few of the old Manchester company had opportunity to return, but when the season began on November 26, 1781, with a performance of *She Stoops to Conquer* two of them, Mrs. Kennedy and Connor, appeared as Kate and Tony Lumpkin. Two nights later Sheridan's *A Trip to Scarborough* was given, and J. S. Munden had his first chance of playing Lory, subsequently one of his most notable parts. He was at this time twenty-three, and had been with the company about a year. During the season he played such parts as Sir Francis Wronghead (*The Provok'd Husband*) Varland (*The West Indian*) Sullen (*The Beaux Stratagem*) and the Clown in *Robinson Crusoe, or Harlequin Friday*, Sheridan's Drury Lane pantomime of the previous year. In the last-named piece Kennedy was Harlequin Friday.

The London Merchant, or George Barnwell might seem heavy fare for New Year's Day, but, as we shall see, Manchester developed a habit of starting the year with a solid slab of moral uplift. Whitlock played Barnwell, and the account was balanced by the farce *All the World's a Stage*, with Munden as Diggory. On January 23 Holcroft's comedy *Duplicity* received its first local performance, and again Whitlock was in the lead as Osborne. The cast also included a newcomer to the company, who played Sir Harry Portland under the name of Romney. This was Samuel Ryley, whose varied career is set out in the many volumes of *The Itinerant* and who darts in and out of the Manchester scene for many years.

Munden's benefit on February 11 gave him his first opportunity of playing Dogberry in *Much Ado About Nothing*; he also sang a comic song 'in the character of Punch', gave 'A Lecture upon Lectures', which introduced 'a Lick at his Own Head', and brought the evening to a close by appearing as Robin in *The Waterman*. For Mrs. Kennedy's benefit, a week earlier, the audience had been promised, as finale, 'A Grand Fete Champetre', with the stage illuminated by one thousand wax lights. A new tragedy by 'A Gentleman of Manchester' (who proved to be Edward Stanley) was performed for the benefit of Mrs. Mason. As the name of this piece was *Elmira*[22] it may be assumed that it was the one laid aside by Robertson in the previous season. The Prologue was spoken by Munden, and after the fourth act an "Ode to Harmony" with music by Richard Wainwright, was introduced.

Austin and Whitlock's other commitments caused an early ending of the season on February 25, when Austin took his benefit before 'a brilliant and crowded audience'. They were back again for Race Week on May 20, when performances were given each night as usual. The managers certainly had plenty to think about, as they were announced to open new theatres in Lancaster and Preston that summer.

The next season did not start until January 1, 1783, when *She Stoops to Conquer* and *The Waterman* were given. A week later a performance of *Venice Preserv'd* was followed by the first appearance in Manchester of George Saville Carey, who gave his lecture on "Mimicry". At the close of *The Merchant of Venice*, in which the principals were Austin (Shylock), Banks (Bassanio), Mrs. William Farren (Portia), and Munden (Launcelot Gobbo), the last-named introduced a song "Four and Twenty Fiddlers" which was to be long associated with him. The performance of *The Foundling* on April 4 was 'for the benefit of Mr. Oliver, late proprietor of the old Theatre Royal, Manchester', meaning, of course, the theatre in Marsden Street.

Prior to this, on Shrove Tuesday, *Chrononhotonthologos* was given, 'as performed at the seat of Sir W. W. Wynne at Wynnstay every Winter'.[23] Everyone not otherwise enjoying a benefit shared in one on April 2. These were Saxton (Gallery-office Keeper), Wood (Check taker), Norbury and Caygill (Bill-givers), Mrs. Burn (House cleaner), and Major, whose duties were unspecified. The company that season included Miss Frodsham, daughter of the 'Garrick of the North'. She later married Samuel Ryley. For her benefit this season she played Imogen. There was also a lady, taking minor parts, who called herself Mrs. Munden, but who was in fact Miss Jones. After bearing Munden several children, she eloped with John Hodgkinson after the visit of this company to Newcastle in 1789, only to be deserted in turn by that gentleman. Hodgkinson subsequently married Miss

Brett and made a considerable name for himself on the American stage.[24] Munden married Miss Butler, who then played leading parts with Austin and Whitlock, and for a spell after Austin's retirement Munden was in partnership with Whitlock before he stepped into Edwin's shoes as a leading comedian in London.

After the customary short season in Race Week, Austin and Whitlock relinquished their interest in Manchester and concentrated on their original circuit. The *Mercury* announced on November 25, 1783, that the Theatre Royal had undergone a thorough and complete repair and had been decorated 'with a variety of New Scenery and Machinery by a very eminent artist'. Further, that 'the Campaign will be opened on Monday next by a company of performers selected from the Theatres Royal, London, Dublin and Edinburgh, under the immediate direction of Mr. Miller (a gentleman whose theatrical abilities need no comment)' winding up with the expectation that the Theatre will 'meet the encouragement and support of every lover of taste, genius and refined entertainment'.

According to Tate Wilkinson, James Miller was 'a man of friendly and honest intentioned principles, and possessed of property, but unfortunately infatuated with two galloping hobby-horses: managing a company of unruly actors, and also much more fond of his own acting than his auditors were' and he goes on to give an amusing anecdote of Miller performing Hamlet at Manchester.[25] He is careful to say 'I believe' before Manchester, and in fact Miller does not appear to have acted during his season as manager. Whatever Miller's personal limitations—and when he died at Worcester on August 14, 1791, he was still actively in control of theatres at Shrewsbury, Worcester and Wolverhampton—his short spell in Manchester is for several reasons of unusual interest.

When the season opened his company contained many performers of earlier years with the addition of Mr. and Mrs. Marshall from York, but on December 10 Thomas Grist made his first Manchester appearance in *The Castle of Andalusia*; an actor who was to become a firm favourite in Manchester over many years. He had made his first appearance anonymously at Drury Lane on October 17, 1775, as Othello, of which performance William Hopkins has the following comment: 'His figure is well enough—a good Voice and Power enough when he knows how to manage it—He is awkward, but it was a very fine first Performance, and, if there is proper care taken with him, he may make an actor'.[26] Writing of him when he was with the York company in 1789, Tate Wilkinson makes a characteristic comment: 'Mr. Grist has received much fame in almost every provincial theatre. He is social in every town with many of the most creditable inhabitants, and is entertaining without recourse to scandal; is in general master of his bottle, and the bottle not master of him—More than I can say of many I wish well'.[27]

When Grist appeared as Othello on December 31 his Desdemona was another newcomer about whom Tate Wilkinson held decided views, Mrs. Robinson. Iago was played by Banks and the Duke was Tony Lebrun, who was to appear larger than life and almost the hero of part of Ryley's *The Itinerant*. Mrs. Robinson had been at Covent Garden for the season of 1782–83. When Wilkinson engaged her at the end of two years at Manchester, he states she had been 'all the prior season the Siddons of Manchester' but he thought more of her comedy than her tragedy, and says of her as the Irish Widow: 'Her figure in the small clothes was neat to a degree of perfection; and her deportment, spirits, and conception of that part was, I think, the best I had then or have since seen', high praise from Wilkinson when one recalls his enthusiasm for Mrs. Jordan. In Manchester, as we shall see, her tragedy was no less highly regarded.

Most interesting of all the newcomers was George Frederick Cooke. 'I come now to a more important era in my theatrical career', he writes in his diary.

Having obtained an engagement for the Manchester Theatre from Mr. James Miller, of Shrewsbury, who was then acting manager, I left Louth on Saturday the 27th December 1783 and arrived at the Lower Swan Inn in Manchester (at that time kept by Dixon) on Tuesday evening the thirtieth. The next day I went to private Lodgings. I made my first appearance on Friday the second of January 1784 in Philotas in The Grecian Daughter and was received with much applause. It was not a very favourable character for a first appearance, for the *then* heroes of Manchester did not seem inclined to participate, or even lend their 'blushing honours' for they were all strange, having only the advantage of me in priority of standing by about a month. This is a courtesy (the choice of a part for a first appearance) which has long been established in well governed theatres; but the Manchester theatre, at the time under Mr. Miller, who had been mostly used to small detachments, was really governed by a cabal, not one of whom are now living, or ever mentioned in theatrical society.[28]

The "Mrs. Cooke" who accompanied him and played minor parts, has not been identified, but it may be assumed she was not Mrs. Cooke.

Cooke was given better opportunities before the end of the season. In *Richard III*, afterwards perhaps his greatest part, he was King Henry to Grist's Richard, but he appeared as Young Marlow, Douglas (in Home's tragedy), Benedick to the Beatrice of Mrs. Robinson, Claudius to Grist's Hamlet, and, on the occasion of the benefit he shared with "Mrs Cooke", Cato in Addison's tragedy. To these parts he added Prospero, Hotspur, Wolsey and Sir Peter Teazle. Benefits seem to have been plentiful that season, and the Cookes enjoyed a second one, when *The Orphan* was performed.

Other benefits for less important members of the company were heralded by advertisements containing the usual mixture of blandishment and frantic appeal. Lebrun and Peile obtained masonic support and a special 'Masonry Song', to music by 'Brother Peile', was sung by 'Brother Craneson'. At Craneson's own benefit he pledged himself 'that no disappointment can possibly happen nor anything promised omitted'. Marshall was less fortunate. He had evidently quarrelled with Miller and announced a concert for his benefit in the Great Room at Owen's Hotel: 'Mr. Marshall having been deprived of the advantages that might have arisen to him from a Benefit in the Theatre humbly hopes that a candid and generous Public will take the Entertainment of that Evening into their Protection'. A fortnight later the breach had been healed and Marshall was able to announce a benefit in the theatre.[29]

Before leaving Miller's season, his first and last in Manchester, notice must be taken of two outside opinions. On May 25 the *Mercury* printed the following:

A gentleman informs us that, accidentally passing through this place on Friday last, he took the opportunity in the evening of being present at the representation of Mr. Sheridan's truly admired comedy The School for Scandal. He had seen the leading characters in the piece performed by the most celebrated personages on the stage, and as he was then unacquainted with the merits of those whose names he read in the Bill, his mind was rather impressed with the idea that the entertainment he would receive would not be so considerable as he wished. But was he deceived in his opinion after the conclusion of a few scenes? The animating and pleasing figure of Mrs. Robinson will surely pre-possess everyone in her favour the moment she appears; but when she displays that elegance and fashion, that life and spirit, the distinguishing characteristics of the part she performed, we feel our minds enlivened by an irresistible impulse of sympathy, and our hearts are forced to confess at the same time that our judgment is convinced that there are few rivals in the theatrical world who have fairer claims to fame and to the reputation of a finished actress. Mr. Grist and Mr. Cooke entered fully into the spirit of their characters, and discovered many conspicuous talents in the line of comedy. Some others of the performers acquitted themselves with great propriety, and our correspondent thinks he should almost censure himself for ingratitude, if he omitted to point out the merits of those in particular from whom he received so ample a degree of pleasure and satisfaction, and who enabled him to spend an evening with real enjoyment, which otherwise (from his want of acquaintance in the place) he must have passed intolerably dull and unpleasant.

In reading eighteenth century newspapers, one must constantly be on guard against an inspired "puff" masquerading as dramatic criticism, but this bears the stamp of honest comment. During this same winter a German, C. G. Küttner, was residing in Manchester and in the form of letters to his own country he subsequently published lengthy books containing his impressions of England. These contain some comments on the English theatres in general and on Manchester. Of the building he says:

The local theatre is small and hardly bigger than the former wooden one at Leipzig, but graceful, warm and comfortable, and the scenes, curtains and effect machines are very good indeed. The proscenium consists of six Corinthian pillars and above it is written: Spectas ut tu spectaberis. In spite of its size, the house has three different entrances, none of which are in connection with the others. It is incomprehensible to me that when the Leipzig theatre was being planned no one thought of the difficulties and the dangers which are a necessary consequence of one general entrance when all the spectators from different seats must pile up on each other. In all the larger theatres I know each section has its own entrance and one can only get from one part to another by going out of the theatre and entering again from the street.

He goes on to point out the advantages of this in case of fire and the way it eases the work of the box-office keeper. He continues:

Alas, over here they do not have the active and economic organisation of the Parterre where for six groschen people of all ranks can enjoy themselves. This section, known as the pit, has benches which can be occupied by people of both sexes.

He found that the theatre, though small, was seldom full:

Many people who have nothing to do, like the students at Leipzig: many officials whose business is over in the evenings; strangers and travellers—all these are lacking here. The common man and the middle class are too busy and the upper classes have other amusements and company, which if they do not prefer to the theatre, do not often go there.

He tells us about the audience.

The gallery is here, as everywhere in England, unbearably unashamed; they throw apples, pomegranates, nut-shells on the stage, in the pit and the boxes; they cry out and make a lot of noise; I know people who refuse to sit in the front seat of the boxes. With ladies they are more polite. Many years ago a flask flew from the gallery into the pit, striking a man's skull. This shrieking and din and all this bad behaviour is difficult in the intervals, but during the play itself the gallery is quieter than I have heard in any other place, and the applause and laughter in the middle of speeches does not last so long that one loses the thread or misses a climax. But here, too, it is the gallery which sets the tone, either booing or applauding or calling for an encore. Of battles and murders are they especially fond, and when the theatre is full of bodies, as at the end of *Hamlet* there is no end to the applause and trumpeting. In England, no one is allowed on the stage.

Küttner does not mention individual actors by name, but we know he must have seen Grist as Hamlet and Richard III, Mrs. Robinson as Isabella (in Southerne's tragedy of that name), Banks as the Ghost and Hollingsworth as First Gravedigger. In line with most foreigners, he thought English actors better in tragedy than comedy. One reason, he thinks, is because 'it is easier to find the true expression of strongly excited feelings and to express strong passions than to imitate the finer politesse, the fine shadings of good humour and the manners and delicacies of polite society'. Although he had been told the Manchester company was one of the best outside London, the poorest French strollers would have known better how to dress and to carry themselves. In comedy the English actors often lacked taste both in dress and deportment; the ladies were better, but often one could not have told the mistress from the maid without the aid of the playbill. It was partly the fault of English comedies, which were still not entirely free from the coarseness of Restoration days, and were wild and turbulent: 'all is movement and the characters are drawn with strong coarse strokes of the pen, and instead of one intrigue there are two, or possibly three'. He finds them mechanical and repetitive.

In tragedy, of course, Shakespeare holds sway, and *Hamlet* is the Englishman's favourite play. 'The text is cut and shortened as is done for the London stage, especially by Garrick'. Many shocking passages and the most ill-formed absurdities are left out, but 'I cannot deny that now and again several worthy passages are lost'. One of these is Polonius's advice to Laertes. He remarks that the Ghost is always played by a leading actor, and that in general the most beautiful and famous speeches are always taken by the best actors, even though the part may be unimportant in other respects (he mentions Jaques). Hamlet's scene with the Ghost impressed him greatly: 'horror and fear overwhelm the theatre. All is attention, and in the whole house among the audience reigns a really gruesome silence. The Ghost speaks without movement or action and yet one cannot imagine anything more pathetic'. The fact that the Ghost was in armour 'and not in black and white' ensured that he was received without 'laughter and childishness'.

Küttner paid special attention to the graveyard scene,

which 'causes no offence to the English and is played completely and without any cuts'. He would not deny that it was full of wit and beauty, 'but there is also much buffooning and absurdity'. He then goes on to describe the notorious removal of 'ten or twelve coats' to the uproar of the gallery, a piece of business which occupied 'fully four minutes'. Five skulls were then produced from the grave followed by a complete skeleton. The reference to Hamlet's madness being no matter in England 'gives rise to a deafening laughter in the whole house'.

The close of the graveyard scene brings further comment.

> Everything is deserted and since the grave is right out in the proscenium it cannot be covered with a curtain. What happens? An attendant comes on with a broom, sweeps all the skulls and bones into the grave, pushes the board back again, lays a carpet on top of this and goes on his way. The English can permit such things without being in the least disturbed.

Richard III was another great favourite with the audience: 'blow follows blow and the spectator is kept breathless till the end'. Küttner is astonished by Shakespeare's historical accuracy, and he admired Grist's acting.

> I have seen the part excellently performed; the actor understood perfectly the strange spirit of this character with all his peculiarities; he shows the character fully as Shakespeare and history represent him, and takes on all the different poses into which this hypocrite used to cast himself. Bruckner and Eckhoff may have played this part very well, but no one understood a really English Richard.

In costume, too, he found this Richard was preferable to the German. He appeared

> neither as the magnificent Bruckner nor in a red uniform like Eckhoff, but as he was or at least as Shakespeare and the

historians paint him: with a crooked back, a growth on his right shin-bone, thick black eyebrows, a black round wig, and his whole figure a trifle bent. All this together in no way makes a ridiculous figure; in fact it is more suited to his character and to the dress of the actual period, which is a kind of old Spanish age. His whole appearance has a certain fearful dignity, in which it is possible to discern the villain and the man of strength and enterprise.

In scenes of death and madness, Küttner clearly found the English insistence on truth to nature a little too much for him. He had never seen 'so fearfully faithful a portrayal' of madness as by Mrs. Robinson in *Isabella*.

She is not like a delicate Frenchwoman who will not give up her good behaviour even in such moments; no, she appears really deathly white, her hair disarrayed and her clothes in real disorder. Her laughter and certain tones of her voice are really horrible and excite unpleasant repulsive feelings.

When it is necessary to die these actors do not provide themselves with chairs and sofas to die worthily, but fall to the ground, often with a violence which makes one anxious for their limbs. One actor imitated the last anguished cries of death with such a horrible veracity and had uttered so many groans which resounded in my breast, that I really shuddered.

Finally, Küttner makes an interesting comparison between English blank verse and the French alexandrine.

Rarely does an actor declaim so perfectly in alexandrines that one does not hear the scansion, however slightly; the blank verse or iambic metre sounds like poetic prose and in the theatre I must listen hard to realise that they are verses; and yet this language has, not only when reading it but also when performing it, much more beauty than prose. It is my opinion that iambic verse is the true language of tragedy and I am much surprised that it has not taken stronger roots in Germany.

He noted that both tragedy and comedy were spoken more slowly than in the French theatre.

Küttner has been treated at length for several reasons: no English editions of his books have appeared; he was writing with experience of the French as well as German theatre on which to form judgment; and, in a period when provincial dramatic criticism had hardly begun, his account is an oasis in a desert of advertisements and playbills.

Miller departed at the end of Race Week, but on July 27 Younger and Mattocks with their Liverpool company gave the first of three performances in Manchester. The programme consisted of two musical pieces, *The Maid of the Mill* and *The Quaker* and the cast included three well-known performers, all new to Manchester: Miss Phillips, subsequently better known as Mrs. Crouch, John Quick and Dick Suett. On August 3, as a mark of friendship for Younger, John Philip Kemble appeared as Tancred in *Tancred and Sigismunda* with Mrs. Mattocks, returning to the theatre after a five years' absence, as Sigismunda and Stephen Kemble making his Manchester debut as Osmond. At the closing performance a week later Mrs. Mattocks again appeared, with Miss Phillips, Suett, Ward and Farren.

Less than a month later, the *Mercury* announced the death of Joseph Younger on September 4, adding a warm tribute: 'A man of the strictest honour and integrity; whose heart was ever prone to acts of charity; and whose actions through life ever stamped him a friendly, honest, upright man'.

Apart from the theatre Manchester had this year—and most years—opportunities of amusement in some of the grotesque exhibitions so typical of the period. In the early weeks there was on view at the Lower Swan Inn 'The Surprizing Dwarf, 22 years old 31 inches high', to which was added 'A Young Lady from Newfoundland'. This exhibition was open each day from eight until eleven, at prices nicely graded to meet social requirements: Ladies and Gentlemen, one shilling; Tradespeople, sixpence; Servants and Children, threepence. There was later a 'Learned Pig' which arrived after a careful "build up"; as 'The Learned Pig has arrived in Warrington and may be expected here next Friday'.

More serious matters were not absent from the town. A Fustian Tax in addition to that already existing aroused great opposition throughout the cotton industry; deputations were sent to London, and representations made in Parliament.[30] Pitt was convinced by their arguments, and the repeal, as will be seen, did not pass without notice in the theatre. The growth and importance of the cotton industry had received further public notice by the passing of an Act to prevent the enticing of workmen or industrial machinery to foreign countries. And in 1784 the distinguished French geologist, Faujas de Saint Fond, was refused admittance to a cotton mill because a French colonel was alleged to have attempted to carry off some drawings. Faujas, incidentally, had some unkind words to say of the Bull's Head where he stayed in Manchester.[31] More happily, the Infirmary raised necessary funds by charging a shilling a head to watch a balloon ascend from its grounds. Nor was it money ill-spent, for the balloon mounted gaily and continued its course to Cromford in Derbyshire.

Although deprived of his partner, Mattocks renewed the responsibility of Manchester as well as Liverpool, and he opened his season on December 29, 1784. In addition to many of Miller's former company, such as Mrs. Robinson, Grist, Cooke, Banks and Hollingsworth, he introduced Stephen Kemble (who was soon joined by his wife), Moss (from Dublin), Mrs. Maddocks (from Norwich), Mrs. Sydney and Fox. With himself and Mrs. Mattocks also, it was a strong company. Cooke and Kemble both appeared in the opening tragedy of *Cleone* and on January 5, 1785, Mrs. Stephen Kemble played Polly to Mattocks's Macheath in *The Beggar's Opera*. Grist again played Hamlet to the Claudius of Cooke, with Kemble as Horatio and Mrs. Kemble as Ophelia. Instead of the farce on several nights Signor Scaglioni introduced 'The Celebrated Dancing Dogs'.

On February 2 M'Nally's comic opera *Robin Hood* was seen for the first time in Manchester. T. Banks painted several new scenes. Fox played Robin Hood, with Hollingsworth as Little John, Mrs. Maddocks as Allen-a-Dale, and Cooke as Baron Fitzherbert disguised as Friar Tuck. T. Banks must not be confused with John Banks, already mentioned as playing the Ghost in *Hamlet*, who became joint manager of the theatre some years later. So far as is known, they were not related, but T. Banks also stayed some years, taking small parts but being busily employed in scene painting.[32]

Unhappily Cooke's appearance in *Robin Hood* was succeeded by one of those upsets which punctuated his career with monotonous regularity. His part of Sir Peter Teazle had been given at Liverpool to Moss, and, when that gentleman departed suddenly soon after reaching Manchester, Mattocks sent the part once again to Cooke, who refused it and left the company, leaving "Mrs. Cooke" behind to finish the season.[33] Evidently Johnson was engaged to take his place, for he appeared on February 11 in the part of Friar Tuck, 'his first on this stage'. M'Nally's opera must have been popular, for it was performed a third time on February 18. Five days later *The Beggar's Opera* was given 'as performed at the Theatre Royal, Haymarket' with the women taking men's parts and vice versa. Mrs. Sydney played Macheath and Fox, Polly. It was repeated on March 2. For her benefit Mrs. Robinson played Portia to the Shylock of Grist, the

Antonio of Kemble and the Bassanio of Banks. Lorenzo
(Fox) and Jessica (Mrs. Sydney) were provided with songs.
When Mattocks took a benefit on March 16 Cumberland's
The Natural Son was first seen in Manchester, and Mrs.
Mattocks also introduced a novelty, *Follies of a Day*, Hol-
croft's version of *Le Mariage de Figaro*, which he had
ingeniously imported from France. Also in the benefit period
was Banks's appearance as King John, Mrs. Kemble's as Jane
Shore, and for the benefit of T. Banks a performance of
Percy, followed by *Harlequin's Invasion* in which T. Banks
played Harlequin and promised 'Harlequin's flight across
the stage from balcony to balcony, and an ascent in a
Tremendous Shower of Fire in the same manner as Signor
Scaglioni's famous English Bull-dog'.

Stephen Kemble's benefit was perhaps the most interesting of all. He announced *The Shipwreck* 'by the author of
George Barnwell' and *Harlequin's Invasion* to conclude
'with brilliant Fireworks', but between these two items was
a musical pastoral, *Philander and Rose*, in two acts, written
by Mrs. Stephen Kemble, to music composed and compiled
by Mr. Cheese, sometime organist of the Collegiate Church.[34]

Mattocks did not make the customary break before Race
Week, but carried the benefit period on until Whit. Advantage was taken of the excitement caused by Sadler's balloon
ascent, much advertised in the *Mercury* about this time
(Balloon Street near Victoria Station remains to-day as a
reminder) and on May 11 and again on May 18 playgoers
were promised on the stage 'an exact representation of
Sadler's Balloon'. *Hamlet* was revived, and Johnson took
Cooke's place as Claudius but Mattocks had saved his best
card to the last. On May 17 he announced that 'Mrs. Siddons
is engaged to perform at this Theatre on Monday and Tuesday next'. The prices went up to five, three and two shillings;
'Servants to keep places must attend at the stage door before

five o'clock'; the doors would open at six and the performance start at seven. The house was to be illuminated with
wax.

It was Mrs. Siddons's first visit to Manchester since her
London triumph, and she opened on May 24 as Isabella, the
part she had performed before the Royal Family at Drury
Lane. Wilkinson went over from York to see her 'and with
great difficulty obtained seats (for Mr. Mattocks would not
interfere in that matter) for our little party, and we saw Mrs.
Siddons perform Isabella that evening and Jane Shore' the
next. Wilkinson is not strictly accurate. He states that Mrs.
Siddons was to perform for six nights, and he gives the two
he saw as Monday and Tuesday, May 23 and 24. These were
as originally announced, but in fact she played on Tuesday
and Wednesday, May 24 and 25.[35]

A month earlier, the delegates sent to agitate for the repeal
of the Fustian Tax, Thomas Walker and Thomas Richardson, arrived back with news of their success. They alighted
at the Bull's Head on April 21 and after a short speech by
Walker, both men were carried on chairs through the streets.
On the following day both ladies and gentlemen wore favours
in the streets, and on May 17 each of the delegates was presented with a silver cup.[36]

The Musical Festival, held at the Concert Hall in Fountain Street on September 21, 22, 23, gave Mattocks another
opportunity of opening the theatre.[37] He engaged Mrs.
Abington to appear on Monday and Tuesday, September 19
and 20, and announced her coming in an unusually long
advertisement. Prices would be raised, wax illumination
used. Mrs. Abington was at this time 48 years old and was
the leading actress of "fine lady" parts. She was the original
Lady Teazle, and had played at Drury Lane for eighteen
years before transferring to Covent Garden in 1782, a move
that gave Elizabeth Farren her great opportunity. Although

so widely known, she had never played in Manchester before. The *Mercury*, which had been strangely silent during Mrs. Siddons's visit, was kinder to Mrs. Abington in its issue of September 27:

> Monday se'nnight, the Theatre was opened here, on account of the Festival of Music, and a brilliant audience assembled to see Mrs. Abington perform Estifania and Lady Racket. To say that she is an inimitable actress is only repeating what has long been allowed; but we cannot help observing that whilst her acting is a genuine copy of Nature, it loses nothing of that vivacity which is so necessary to the support of character upon the stage. Tuesday evening she performed the Widow Belmour, and Mrs. Mattocks the part of Mrs. Lovemore, to a very crowded audience, who repeatedly testified the great pleasure they received from the united abilities of two such admirable actresses.

It may be worth mention that the announcement for the second night stated the normal prices, but whether this was a printer's lapse or an indication that Mrs. Abington's drawing power was less than expected, it is not possible to say. In the same week Mrs. Crouch, whom we last saw as Miss Phillips, and who was singing at the Festival, played one night at the theatre. One of her pieces was *Rosina*, an operetta by Mrs. Brooke about which Küttner had written with enthusiasm. There seemed to be no end to theatrical attractions in 1785, for on September 26 Charles Macklin appeared as Shylock, and on September 28 as Sir Archy MacSarcasm in his own *Love à la Mode*. Macklin, who came over from Ireland for this engagement, was said to be 87 years old. Another Festival singer, Signora Sestini, made appearances at this period in musical pieces.

In November, the 'Little Devil and his Company' gave their pantomimic and callisthenic entertainment, *An Olio, or the Amusements of Sadler's Wells*. The Little Devil (whose real name was Paulo Redige) was announced to 'dance with wooden shoes on the rope, break them in the air, and alight on the rope in the most astonishing manner'. La Belle Espagniola would dance a hornpipe on the rope without a pole, and follow this with a Spanish Fandango with castanets, still on the rope. There was tumbling by other members of the party, and a final pantomime, *Harlequin Foundling*, which introduced 'the favourite Skeleton Scene' with alterations and additions never attempted but by the Little Devil and Company'. Their final performance was on November 30.

Mattocks did not start his regular season until January 3, 1786. The company included many of the previous season's performers, though Mrs. Robinson had joined Tate Wilkinson, the Kembles were in Scotland, and "Mrs. Cooke" and Lebrun were also absent. To fill the gaps, Whitfield came to share the leading business with Grist, and other newcomers were Mr. and Mrs. Kelly, Miss Evans, Mrs. Whitfield and Mrs. Warrall,[39] who took singing parts. Mrs. Farren returned once more, and from Ireland, recommended to Mattocks by Charles Macklin, came William M'Cready. M'Cready (or Macready—the *Monthly Mirror* uses both forms) was to have very mixed experiences in Manchester before his career ended, but now, in 1786, his engagement and that of Miss Birch were by far the most important aspects of this Manchester season. M'Cready soon made up his mind about Miss Birch: on April 7, the last night before the Easter holidays, the two shared a benefit, when M'Cready played Bob Acres and Miss Birch Julia in *The Rivals*. M'Cready published in the *Mercury* of April 11 a letter of thanks, assuring his supporters 'it shall be his constant study to merit a continuance of such liberal protection'. Two months later, on June 17, 1786, William McCready and Christina Ann Birch were married at the Collegiate Church. The signature in the register introduced a third variant in spelling.

Reverting to the season—the programme on January 11 consisted of *I'll Tell You What* and *The Mogul Tale,* the first two dramatic efforts of Mrs. Inchbald, both first produced at the Haymarket in the previous summer. *The Mogul Tale* had as sub-title *A Flight in an Air Balloon,* and this may have encouraged a second performance within a week, this time as an afterpiece to the inevitable *George Barnwell.* There was never any difficulty in turning stock pieces to topical advantage, and a good example was on January 20 when a revival of *Robinson Crusoe* concluded with 'a Representation (in Miniature) of the Procession of the Repeal of the Fustian Tax'. By February 1 this was having its third performance. On February 7 the *Mercury* reported 'We hear that the men who occasioned the disturbance at the Theatre on Monday last were brought before Thomas Butterworth Bayley and Michael Bentley, Esquires, two of His Majesty's Justices of the Peace, when on their expressing their error, begging pardon for their conduct and promising good behaviour for the future, they were dismissed without further prosecution'. Between the play and the farce on February 15 there was a concerto on the harpsichord 'by Mr. Peck, a pupil of the late Mr. Bach' (doubtless Johann Christian, who settled in England and died in 1782). Whitfield played Lear and Orlando, and Grist was seen once again as Hamlet. This version, unlike that seen by Küttner, omitted the gravediggers, and was no doubt Garrick's adaptation, played at Drury Lane during his last four seasons there.

The Little Devil and his Company returned to provide the afterpiece for several performances in February, and in mid-March the benefits began. Mrs. Mattocks had two pieces new to Manchester, Burgoyne's *The Heiress* and a pantomime, *Queen Mab,* with scenes painted by T. Banks. The latter revived *Tamerlane* with Whitfield in the title part, and followed with an old favourite *Harlequin Doctor Faustus,* which had seen good service everywhere since Rich first produced it. T. Banks promised many antics as usual. More daring, Kelly brought forward a tragedy of his own writing *Almira* (April 28) with a Prologue 'by a person of fashion' spoken by Grist, and an Epilogue 'by a Gentleman of Manchester' spoken by M'Cready. This Epilogue, the *Mercury* assured its readers, had 'a claim to public attention, as it conveys a striking picture of our manufactures, and a handsome eulogium on the town and trade of Manchester'.

Mattocks continued his previous year's policy of carrying the season on, and of introducing a succession of notable visitors. Mrs. Crawford was the first, and he let it be known that although Tate Wilkinson had announced "London prices" for her visit to York, Manchester would have the privilege of seeing her at ordinary charges. He kept to this intention during the visits of Mrs. Jordan, Jack Johnstone and Charles Bannister which followed, and did not put up the prices even for the visit of Mrs. Siddons and John Philip Kemble in July. It becomes clear in the light of after events that Mattocks was making a frantic effort to keep his head above water. In Gilliland's *Dramatic Mirror* it is stated that Mrs. Siddons's six nights produced £64, £89, £92, £67, £77 and £78, figures which are not very remarkable but should be judged with reference to ordinary prices, whereas higher prices were usually in operation on her provincial tours.[40] During this engagement she played Lady Randolph in *Douglas* and Calista in *The Fair Penitent.* In addition to her brother John, James Aickin and Barrymore, neither of whom had played in Manchester before, supported her.

Although neither he nor anyone else knew it at the time, Mattocks's spell as manager at Manchester had ended. On January 2, 1787, he announced in the *Mercury* that 'the Theatre would open on January 3rd if the performers Mr.

Mattocks had engaged from London, Bath, etc., arrive in time'. The season did, in fact, start on January 5, but by that time Mattocks had handed over to a new partnership. On January 9 Messrs. Connor and Sydney informed the public that 'they had taken over the responsibility of the Theatre Royal when its concerns were materially deranged and they ask for the indulgence and co-operation of the Public; they promise every attention and the provision of good plays, and satisfaction in every way'. The precise date of their taking over may be inferred from a further announcement at the end of the season when they expressed their readiness to settle claims from January 2 to May 28.

The company was very different from that of the previous year. John and T. Banks, Webb, Maddocks, Hollingsworth, Mrs. Sydney and Mrs. Maddocks returned, but Grist, Whitfield, M'Cready, Fox, Johnson and Kelly had gone, as well as Mrs. Farren, Mrs. Warrall and, of course, Mrs. Mattocks. Among the newcomers were Hamerton and Browne, both from Dublin, Hurst, an older actor who had played at Drury Lane, Mrs. Cornellys and Mrs. Emery. Samuel Ryley came back after adventures set out in *The Itinerant* and he had Mrs. Ryley (whom we last saw as Miss Frodsham) with him. Compared with earlier seasons it bears a makeshift appearance, no doubt the result of Mattocks's financial difficulties. Hamerton and Browne shared the leading business: Hamerton played Othello, Bassanio, Lord Gayville and Charles Surface: Browne was seen as Hamlet, Iago, Posthumus and Sir Peter Teazle. Mrs. Emery played Desdemona, Imogen, and Mrs. Cornellys, Lady Teazle and Catharine. Connor played only minor parts and Sydney was not on the stage.

On March 4 Browne announced in the *Mercury* that 'in consequence of a very oppressive and cruel attempt of Mr. Daly to distress him, the managers had granted him an early benefit, on Monday, March 12th'. This was followed a month later by notice that Browne (by permission of the managers) would that day (April 3) 'deliver a Literary Divertimento consisting of a choice selection of English Readings'. Songs would be sung by Mrs. Shepley and Waterhouse (the latter the successor to Fox as singing man in the company). Tickets were two shillings and sixpence boxes, and two shillings pit. One assumes the gallery remained closed. Whatever else had changed T. Banks was still full of ideas for his benefit. *Cato* was performed, with John Banks in the title part, and in Act IV a funeral procession was introduced, to the music of the Dead March in Saul. There followed a 'compiled Pantomime Magic and Mirth'. T. Banks undertook to leap through the stage door and also 'leap through A Grand Firework representing a Resplendent Sun'. As Harlequin, he also promised 'a new dying scene'. Ryley imitated birds at his own benefit, but for his wife's he introduced a new song 'by Mr. Cowdry of Chester', called 'The Learned Pig's Levee, a Chiming, Grunting, Snorting Rhapsody'. This song, with various adaptations, was to serve Ryley well for many years.[41]

For Race Week Mrs. Robinson reappeared and played Isabella, Jane Shore and the Irish Widow, ending with Margaret of Anjou to the Warwick of John Banks in *The Earl of Warwick* on June 8. In the *Mercury* of June 12 Connor and Sydney returned thanks for the past and promised good things in the future.

A new season was heralded in the *Mercury* of November 6, 1787, with the announcement that the season would open on November 12 'with a favourite tragedy in which Miss Eccles, from Theatre Royal, Haymarket, would perform.[42] The house had been 'completely refitted and ornamented with entire new scenery by Mr T Banks' and there was 'an extensive and fashionable new modern Wardrobe'.

The special mention of Miss Eccles, whose stay at the Haymarket had been brief and undistinguished, suggests that the managers had little new with which to tempt playgoers. Miss Eccles played Belvidera in *Venice Preserv'd* to the Jaffier of Browne on November 14 (the season appears to have begun on this date) but for the rest her leading parts were few.[43] Charles Wood and Mrs. Peile, both singers, were new, and so was Kippling, who took over the Hollingsworth comedy parts such as Dogberry. Tony Lebrun returned to join his friend Ryley.

Much interest was worked up for the production of *Oroonoko,* Southerne's adaptation of Mrs. Behn's novel. Thomas Clarkson had started his campaign against the slave trade, and Southerne's play acquired a topical significance. The *Mercury* on November 27 printed a long piece, asserting that the play 'besides its poetical Merit derives a strong Interest from its foundation in Truth'. Mrs. Behn had known 'the unfortunate Prince' and the play verified the remark frequently made 'that the Powers of Fiction can add nothing to the Force of the authenticated Miseries produced by the African Slave Trade'. Readers were assured that 'all the Comic Scenes which have long disgraced this most excellent play are entirely expunged'. *Oroonoko* was performed on November 28 with Browne in the leading part, and with a new Prologue, which the *Mercury* printed in full on December 4. The play was repeated on New Year's Day, 1788. A week later a petition against the slave trade was printed, and the issue for February 5 gave a list of addresses (mostly inns) where the petition could be signed. Between these dates, on January 29 the *Mercury* printed a piece "The African Slave", spoken by George Saville Carey at the theatre eight days earlier. Carey and Moses Kean, giving their 'System of Mimicry' had provided the afterpiece on several nights about this time.

To turn back for a moment, Mrs. Smith[44] (from Theatre Royal, York) appeared for the first time on December 5 when she performed Beatrice to the Benedick of Browne. This must have been her favourite part, as Wilkinson tells us she chose it for her debut in his company. On the same night *Rosina* was revived once more, with Mrs. Peile as the principal.

Early in December, the theatre had to face opposition from Astley's Circus, which established itself at the Riding House in Tib Street. Six performances were announced, readers being assured that Astley had shortly to be in Paris, but he was still in Manchester when the new year opened. Another attempted competitor, Charles Dibdin, was less successful. He made a long announcement of his appearance on January 15, 1788, at the Great Room, Bull's Head, where he promised 'Readings, interspersed with Music, in two parts, with an Exordium'. He stayed three nights with little success.

On January 30 Miss Eccles played Julia in the first Manchester performance of Jephson's play of that name, and when *Hamlet* was revived on February 5 Browne was again the Prince, Mrs. Sydney, Ophelia, and Kippling, Polonius. The Gravedigger scene was restored, with Ryley and Lebrun providing what must have been an entertaining combination. Or perhaps not, for Ryley was granted an early benefit on February 8 'in consequence of his late misfortune'. To which of Ryley's many misfortunes this relates is not known. When Kippling took his benefit on March 11 he announced, in addition to *The Suspicious Husband,* an adaptation of Ben Jonson's *The Alchemist* called *The Tobacconist* and, according to the advertisement, made expressly for Kippling by Colman[45]. An Epilogue, it was stated, would be spoken 'by Mr. Kippling riding on an ass'.

On February 26 the *Mercury* contained an advertisement

that Mrs. Sydney was about to retire from the stage and open a boarding school at her house near the Old Quay. This was repeated many times and Mrs. Sydney's 'last Benefit' was announced for April 7, when T. Banks painted new scenery for *The Rivals*. The regular season closed on April 25, but on May 5 at the Great Room, Bull's Head, Kippling performed his 'agreeable Gallimaufry', which included a recital of Cowper's poem "John Gilpin".

The great event of Race Week was the reappearance of George Frederick Cooke,[46] who performed *Hamlet* on May 13, with Mrs. Sydney as Ophelia, Banks as the Ghost and Ryley and Lebrun as Gravediggers. Plays were performed every night that week, but no casts are known or whether Cooke made more than one appearance. On May 27 there was a brief mention that Jack Johnstone and Wright Bowden[47] were coming shortly, and this was followed up on June 3. They appeared on June 11 in *Love in a Village,* supported by some of the regular company. The number of their performances is not certain, but Johnstone took a benefit on June 17. Bowden afterwards obtained fame at Covent Garden as a vocalist.

Before the new season opened the theatre was in use on several occasions. On July 28 Mrs. Peile, who 'had declined Summer Engagement owing to indisposition' held a concert for her benefit, at which most of Manchester's leading musicians performed. On September 8 Mr. Buckley provided a morning performance of *Acis and Galatea* and on October 3 a company under Hamilton and Brett started a season which lasted several weeks.

Sydney withdrew from management before the next season started, and Connor's new partner was John Banks. For the season which opened on December 29, 1788, Mrs. Taylor, formerly Mrs. Robinson, returned to take leading roles, and there were newcomers—Williams, Penn, Seymour, Creswell; and Mrs. Edwards from Norwich. On December 31 Williams played Orlando to Mrs. Taylor's Rosalind and Creswell's Touchstone, and on January 7[48] Penn appeared as Macbeth, with Banks as Macduff, Spragg as Malcolm, Williams as Banquo and Mrs. Taylor as Lady Macbeth. Penn played other parts, including Prospero, Friar Laurence, but does not appear in announcements after mid-February, save that a benefit is advertised in March and then postponed because of a Ball celebrating the King's recovery in health. This benefit does not seem to have taken place. One may hazard a guess that Grist, who suddenly reappears in the company in February, was engaged to take Penn's place. He took a benefit on March 9, playing Wolsey to the Henry VIII of Banks, the Queen of Mrs. Taylor and the Anne Bullen of Mrs. Edwards. Williams was off the stage for five weeks with a broken leg, but Seymour was also available for leading parts and played Romeo, George Barnwell and Cromwell.

The performance of *George Barnwell* on February 24 was followed by 'A Superb Spectacle' by 'Les Quartres Fils Hemond', a display of 'Broadsword and Battle Axe by Mons. Durenci and Mons. Boimason', a single combat as performed by these two gentlemen at Paris. They were also present on March 4, for *Harlequin Mungo* for which the music was composed and selected by the local musician, Robert Barber. The scenery and machinery for this were 'under the Direction of Mr. Luppino of Theatre Royal, Covent Garden.' The pantomime was repeated a week later, and on March 20 the visiting swordsmen took a benefit, when there was an additional attraction in 'The Famous Spaniard from Sadler's Wells, who will perform feats, throw a somerset backward and discharge two pistols at the same time'.

After these excitements the ordinary benefit period continued. Mrs. Taylor chose *The Regent* which 'had been kept from the public on account of a recent Melancholy Circumstance' and on Seymour's benefit night (March 27) he promised 'the Original Transparencies and Devices as appeared on the night of the 19th on the occasion of the Celebrations for His Majesty's Recovery'. There was a 'Grand Chorus of God Save the King'. Seymour also recited Gray's "Elegy".

Both Banks and Connor contrived to be equally original. Banks followed *A Bold Stroke for a Husband* with 'A Grand Tragic Pantomimic Entertainment' on the subject of Don Juan. The songs, duets and choruses were by Mr. Reeve and the music composed by Mons. Gluck. Luppino was responsible for the 'Scenery, Machinery, Devices and Transparencies'. Connor had *The Orphan* in which Chamont was played 'by a Gentleman of Manchester, his first time on any stage'. Before the farce could be seen 'a Sparring Match by Mr. Mendoza (who fought Humphries) and another celebrated Pugilist'. On May 4 Mrs. Taylor appeared as Hamlet for the benefit of her husband, and another relatively minor actor, Richards, brought forward for his benefit a new comedy, *The Merry Men of Kent,* written 'by a Young Gentleman of Manchester', with the ever-popular *Rosina* as afterpiece and a glee composed by Barber. Ryley wrote a new piece *The Civilian* for his wife's benefit and Haigh, violinist in the theatre orchestra, composed or selected the overture and songs. Ryley also sang "The Cries of Manchester".

Commencing on May 18, Joseph George Holman fulfilled an engagement of six nights. He began with Romeo, and also included Orestes, Benedick, Tancred and Macbeth, his leading lady in each play being Mrs. Taylor. Then Thomas King came for a short engagement, which terminated on June 12 with his benefit performance of *The Beaux Stratagem* and *The Critic,* in which King played two of his famous parts, Scrub and Puff. This was intended as the end of the season; it proved—as the *Mercury* explained on June 23—the last performance in the building.

> On Friday morning, a little after 12 o'clock, an alarming fire broke out in the Theatre Royal, in this town, which spread with such fury that in a quarter of an hour from its first appearance the building was an entire blaze, and there appeared not the least possibility of preserving anything. The damage has not yet been estimated, but from its being reduced to a mere shell, and every article destroyed, we should suppose it to exceed £3000, to which amount the insurance nearly extends. The steady attention of the 3rd regiment of Dragoon Guards, and the kind assistance of the magistrates and gentlemen deserve particular thanks. Considerable damage was done to the occupiers of the houses and warehouses adjoining, from which it was thought necessary to remove the goods.

Harrop, who was owner of the *Mercury* as well as lessee of the theatre, added an announcement thanking the military and other helpers for their valuable assistance, and in the same issue was a notice calling the proprietors together for a general meeting on very particular business. Other meetings followed, the final one on July 28 evidently approving plans for rebuilding, for the work began almost at once on the old site and was virtually completed by the end of the year. On February 9, 1790, the *Mercury* announced that the opening would be on February 15. The public was also informed that 'four large stoves in Addition to the usual Number of Fires have been constantly kept both Night and Day for the six weeks past to make the Theatre both warm and dry'.

It seems strange at first sight that when the theatre was destroyed the chance was not taken to build one more in keeping with Manchester's growing size and importance. Finance may have played its part, and also the restricted nature of the site. Moreover, although a survey made at

Christmas, 1788, had shown that Manchester's population had more than doubled in fifteen years, we do not know whether this increase had been reflected in the theatre audiences. If the policy seems over-cautious, it was no more blameworthy than the optimism of the builders of the next Theatre Royal, who spread themselves and created a mill-stone for their own necks. That the new theatre was too small soon became evident.

III

1790—1800

FOR THE OPENING of the new building on February 15, 1790, there was another change in management, Connor having withdrawn. His place as partner to Banks was taken by Thomas Ward, who has already figured prominently in these records since his first appearance under Whitley at the Marsden Street Theatre. He was to remain joint manager of the first Theatre Royal until it closed in 1807, and to serve later as manager for W. T. Lewis of the second Theatre Royal in Fountain Street. In all, his span of activity on the Manchester stage covered almost half-a-century. He was to have his moments of unpopularity, but the public would hardly have supported him over so many years if he had been no more competent than some of the pamphleteers suggested. A rhymester who called himself 'C. Censor' published in 1793 *The Thespian Mirror or Poetical Strictures,* setting out in doggerel verse his views on the Manchester performers of that date. Of Ward he writes:

> Kind fortune tho' now and then guilty of teazing,
> Has rendered him affable, sprightly and pleasing.
> In the walks of light comedy few can excel him,
> But to undertake tragedy nought should impel him.

His failings, the rhymester admits, 'are few when compared with his numerous merits' and although he writes of 'his dissonant voice' he continues that he knows 'the road to the heart and to make it rejoice'. Despite the views of 'C. Censor', Ward seems to have enjoyed considerable success in tragedy in the earlier part of his career, though throughout he was better fitted for comedy. Even the pamphleteers had little to say against his acting; it was against Ward as a manager that their shafts were directed.

Ward had a great asset in his wife, an actress of more than ordinary ability, whose only fault as a performer was the common one of playing youthful parts long after her age permitted the illusion. She appeared with a good deal of success in London, and her last appearance in Manchester did not take place until 1816. Their daughter, who appeared during some seasons as will be seen, married a noted Manchester surgeon. The new partnership was a family affair, for John Banks had married Mrs. Kniveton, sister of Mrs. Ward. About Mrs. Kniveton 'C. Censor' can find nothing good to say, but Tate Wilkinson says 'she was a lady of established merit, and well-known in the theatrical world; was a very handsome woman and a good actress'.[49]

Oddly enough, neither announcement (apart from the date) nor playbill of the opening night has survived though Procter tells us that Banks spoke an inaugural address and Ryley sang a song he had composed for the occasion.[50] There were many changes in the company. Congdon came from Margate and stayed for several seasons, though if any reliance can be placed on 'C. Censor' his abilities were not outstanding. Barrett, who was stated (incorrectly, so far as can be ascertained) to have been manager for many years at Norwich, Mrs. Freeman, Mrs. Rivers and Mrs. Davis were other newcomers.

In advance of Barrett's benefit the *Mercury* printed a long and enthusiastic notice of the company, and of Barrett in particular. It commended Banks for collecting so good a company (there was no mention of Ward) and went on to praise Banks whose 'merits as a performer are well-known and his conduct in private, as well as public life will always, no doubt, produce him a good harvest from a generous and indulgent public'. The company was 'the most regular and indeed the most correct in their business we have seen for some years'. Barrett's performances of Ranger, Charles Surface, Lord Townley, Hamlet and Belcour, 'do him infinite honour' and indeed 'we do not remember so universal a performer'. Nor are the ladies forgotten: 'Mrs. Rivers is an excellent figure, has a melodious voice and expressive countenance; Mrs. Freeman is an excellent singer, and Mrs. Davis is particularly happy in "The Romp" '.[51]

From what we know of the players, this seems over-generous as a view of the company, but Wilkinson expresses similar views about Mrs. Rivers, and in comedy Barrett became an established favourite in Manchester until his death in 1795. As a further example of 'C. Censor' and his verses the following may be noted:

Behold Little Barrett; the father of smiles,
Possessed of a secret that sorrow beguiles;
From the seat of his wit to the tip of his chin
His face is a compound of laughter and grin;
His voice and appearance accord with his spirit;
And equally serves to establish his merit,
With spirits on fire and body tip-toe,
He looks like a Bantam preparing to crow;
An amorous sparrow just come from its nest,
Or an undersized turkey erecting his crest.

One is still left wondering what his Hamlet was like. Stanton, member of a well-known theatrical family, was better known as a scene-painter than as actor, and for his benefit he exhibited during the pantomime several 'Grand Perspectives', giving views of the New Bayley Prison and 'a distinct inside view of the Cells', as well as one of St. Peter's Church, then being built, and showing what it would look like when finished. For their benefits both managers selected plays new to Manchester, Banks giving Colman's *The Battle of Hexham,* and Ward, *The Dramatist* by Reynolds.

During this summer the Hon. John Byng paid the first of two visits to Manchester and recorded his impressions in his diary. For the theatre he cannot help us, as both visits were in the close season. He prints an advertisement for 'The Bridgwater Arms' whose claims he did not find carried out in practice. A great noisy hotel, he calls it 'whose clamour, bell-ringing and want of attendance wou'd drive a man wild'. Outside the hotel, things were no better: 'I wander'd about this great nasty manufacturing town; looking exactly like Spitalfields and those environs; their exchange is a handsome building, but crowded up in a low situation'. In the Collegiate Church the singing was too bad to be endured, but he wandered at will in Chetham's College and Library. What he called the New Town was 'hourly increasing in buildings of the better sort' and he mentions the Infirmary, the chapels, and the assembly rooms for dancing, well-built and bespeaking opulence and an increasing trade. But he exclaims 'Who but a merchant cou'd live in such a hole!' Byng was not short of prejudices, but he was an acute and candid observer and we would wish he had contrived a visit when the theatre was open.[52]

The next season began on October 18, 1790, and introduced what appeared a much stronger company. Mrs. Taylor returned after two years absence, and Mr. and Mrs. Swendall began a long association with the theatre.[53] Bristow from Bath, Mrs. Powell, another of Mrs. Ward's sisters, and Errington also appeared. Of more potential interest was the coming of a young man calling himself Merchant, who was in fact Thomas Dibdin, the son of Charles. Young Dibdin was at this time only nineteen, but he sets out in his *Reminiscences* the qualifications he could offer: 'Sing Poor Jack, paint scenes, play the fiddle, write a farce, get up a pantomime, attempt Sir Francis Gripe, Apollo (Midas), Mungo (The Padlock), Darby (The Poor Soldier), Capt. Valentine (The Farmer), Polonius (Hamlet), not to mention all dialects such as the Irishman in "Rosina" or anything else with French or German characters, which I always played in Manchester'. Dibdin states that he was in the company which opened the new house, but in fact he joined it for the second season.[54]

Dibdin played some of the parts he mentions during his Manchester seasons, but when *The Farmer* was given before Christmas the Valentine was a newcomer, Kelly, who came from Dublin and was a brother of Michael Kelly. Two serious pantomimes *The Death of Capt. Cook* and *The Death of General Wolfe* emphasised Manchester's tendency to take its pleasures seriously, even at Christmas. Early in the New Year Wright Bowden played Capt. Macheath during a special engagement, and in the same month Bates returned to the company after a long absence and opened as Sharp in *The Lying Valet*. 'C. Censor' thought well of him: 'Bates is a favourite of men and of gods' and other lines of commendation appear in the *Thespian Mirror*. It was Bates also, according to Dibdin, who said that it rained so constantly at Manchester that one could imagine its good genius was ever shedding tears over it. When Bates took his benefit on April 12, and chose *Twelfth Night*, that most popular of comedies was surprisingly announced 'never acted here'.

Another newcomer that season was Tyrrell, whom Dibdin calls 'as hearty a fellow and nearly as good an Irish actor as ever trod the boards'. Like Swendall, he settled down to become a constant member of the company over many years.

For Race Week Cooke returned, and Mrs. Ward, who had been playing at Drury Lane, renewed her association with Manchester, which was to end only on her retirement in 1816. As Cooke was also persuaded to rejoin the regular company, Banks and Ward opened their new season on November 14, 1791, with much stronger forces. Cooke could never be anything but a trial to any management. The announcements of his sudden 'indispositions' can hardly have deluded the audience, and it is some indication of his outstanding ability and genuine popularity that, at a period when the public was quick to note and resent any discourtesy towards them by the players, he could always placate his audience without much difficulty. Dibdin says 'Cooke was perhaps a greater favourite in Manchester than in any other town in England; his powers of acting were at th's time at their zenith; his love of conviviality still superior to his power of acting'. Dibdin tells us he lodged next door to him 'and acted as agent and counsel for him in disputes with the managers'.

Richardson, a newcomer from Bath, had been on the stage only a year, having previously concerned himself in business at Worcester, but it was said his original intention was to enter the Church, which may account for the comment of 'C. Censor' who warned him:

Remember in this most critical age,
What does for the pulpit will not for the stage.

The same writer also took him to task for self-admiration and other blemishes. As always, such criticism must be taken with caution, for 'C. Censor' strikes one as glib rather than knowledgeable on many occasions and had many bees in his bonnet. Where contemporary comment is so sparse, however, it cannot be passed over entirely. After his Manchester engagement Richardson appeared at Norwich and Covent

Garden with some success. Mrs. Simpson also came from Bath where, according to Tate Wilkinson, she had been a great favourite. 'She is a very pleasant, elegant actress', he says of her, 'both in tragedy and comedy, but not powerful nor great as the commanding breath of Kings; but she is always sure to gain the good word of gentlemen and ladies, and all the parts of a good-natured house'.[55] She stayed only one season in Manchester before joining Wilkinson. Mention must also be made of Miss Daniels, if only because she met Cooke at Manchester and was later to marry him and later still to obtain from the court a decree of nullity. She took singing parts, and was another for whom 'C. Censor' could find nothing good to say. Dibdin, however, calls her 'a good singer and a good girl'.

Early in the new season, on November 23, Mrs. Inchbald's latest comedy *Next Door Neighbours* was produced, but the first notable event was the performance of *Wild Oats*, a comedy by O'Keeffe, which was to become a stock favourite everywhere and to enjoy London revivals down to the days of Charles Wyndham. We may assume its immediate popularity in Manchester from the many revivals within a brief spell. The cast included Ward, Cooke, Barrett, Banks, Davis, Bates and Mrs. Simpson. Another play by O'Keeffe, *The Beggar on Horseback*, and Dudley's comic opera *The Woodman* were among other productions, and on Whit-Monday there was a special performance of *The Rivals* in aid of the Infirmary. To end the season there was another night given over to charity, this time the Lying-In Hospital, which had been founded two years earlier. The programme was impressive: first *The Jealous Wife* with Cooke and Mrs. Simpson as principals; then Handel's *Grand Coronation Anthem,* in which the invaluable Mrs. Shepley was chief soloist; and finally *The Agreeable Surprise*. 'The Gods and Goddesses at our Theatre', noticed the

Mercury, had insisted on "God Save the King" being played before they would permit the play to go on.

The theatre was opened for a brief season in September and Mrs. Taylor appeared. For the regular season Grist returned once more and there was also Miss Cleland, who, Tate Wilkinson tells us, had 'a good person, a good understanding and a great deal of whim'. She was very adequate in parts requiring comprehension from the performer, he considered, but she should avoid attempting to ensnare the audience with 'the amiable, the gentle, the tender or the great'.[56] At Manchester she played Gertrude in *Hamlet* on New Year's Day, 1793, to the Hamlet of Cooke, with Tyrrell as the King, Grist as the Ghost, Barrett as Polonius, Bates as First Gravedigger, Richardson as Laertes, and Miss Corneleys as Ophelia.

A farce by William Macready, *The Irishman in London* seems to have been successful for it was played three times within a brief period. A local singer appeared as Lionel to the Clarissa of Miss Daniels, and was summarily dealt with by 'C. Censor,' whose *Thespian Mirror,* so often quoted in these pages, was published in this year. Cooke played Prospero in *The Tempest* with Banks as Caliban, Mrs. Francis as Miranda and Miss Daniels as Ariel.

This was 1793 and the death of Louis XVI on January 21 brought patriotic fervour to boiling point. An effigy of Paine was publicly burned, meetings were held, loyal addresses passed, and witch hunts for real or alleged Jacobins were instigated. This diehard's paradise was naturally reflected in the theatre. On January 29, for the first time for many years, the theatre remained closed on the anniversary of King Charles's death. On February 11 *Henry V* was revived, with Cooke as the King, and when the benefits started, advantage was taken of the prevailing trend. Mrs. Powell chose *Henry V* again on February 27, followed by a farce *Warlike*

Preparations which included battle scenes. When Congdon took his benefit on March 1 and *Julius Cæsar* was performed it was announced that "God Save the King" would be played 'for the 57th time this season'. Not satisfied with this Congdon also included *Manchester Loyalty; or the Constitutional Association* during which would be exhibited 'A Superb Painting (by a Gentleman of Manchester) Representing the King in Full Stature'. Appropriate songs, such as "The Good Subjects of Old England" and "Rouse Britannia's Warlike Throng" were sung, and also a Constitutional Glee composed by Merchant (as Dibdin was still known in Manchester). The latter also wrote for Barrett's benefit a 'poetical, comical, vocal, rhetorical Interlude' called *Snip's Return from the Camp; or The Manchester Marine*. Barrett had written a song "Good King George" which he sang himself, and copies of which were distributed at the door.

Dibdin does not appear to have done very well in the way of parts, but he was making himself useful in other ways. 'Whenever the painting room required a tenant' he tells us, he was employed there, turning out new scenery for *The Tempest* and *Richard Coeur de Lion* among other things. For the benefit he shared with Williamson on March 15 he followed *Julius Caesar* with a farce of his own, *Sunshine after Rain*, and also sang a comic song of his own composition called "The Manchester Dyer".[57] Novelty, usually so essential at benefits, was evidently overruled by other considerations this year, for Cooke again revived *Henry V,* after which he recited Collins's "Ode on the Passions" and concluded with a loyal address to the audience.

Although April 26 had been announced as the last night before the Races, the theatre again opened on May 13 for the first performance of Samuel Ryley's comic opera *Roderick Random* based on Smollett's novel, with music composed by Grimshaw, organist of St. John's Church. For the time being

Ryley's wanderings had ceased and he was installed as land-
lord of the Angel Tavern in Oldham Street. The full
strength of the company turned out for this occasion, and
Ryley himself played Strap. Two nights later there was a
performance 'for the Benefit of such Poor Persons within the
Townships of Manchester and Salford as, under the pres-
sure of the present Circumstances, ought to be so relieved'.
The Provok'd Husband was given, with Grist as Townley.
During Race Week Bowden paid another visit, playing
Comus, and Macheath to the Polly of Miss Daniels.

Meanwhile, other things in the world of entertainment
had been brought to public notice. Astley had been paying
one of his "brief" visits, which as usual lasted a long time,
and then on April 16 the *Mercury* printed a long advertisement, headed 'The New Circus in Chatham Street at the
Top of Piccadilly will open in the first week of June, 1793'.
There followed an impressive list of singers, pantomimists,
musicians, painters who had been engaged. Merchant was
among the painters, the theatre was further represented by
Davis, Williamson, and Miss Valois, and such names as
Moorhead, Hughes, Sudlow, Clough and Ridings figured
among the musicians. On May 28 the *Mercury* printed a cer-
tificate that the New Circus was sound in structure, and on
June 4 it was announced that Bates, prior to departing for
America, would produce *Gil Blas* at the Circus on June 25.
The cast of this included Merchant, Williamson, Davis, and
Miss Valois in addition to Bates.[58]

At the theatre Mrs. Siddons played a short season before
the regular season opened. As always she included *Isabella*,
with Cooke as Biron, and on November 23 'for the benefit of
the fund for the warmer clothing of the English soldiery in
France' she was seen as Portia to the Shylock of Cooke, with
Tyrrell as Antonio. For the new season starting on December 26, 1793, Mrs. Taylor returned as leading lady, Iliff

came from the Haymarket and Mr. and Mrs. Hatton also joined the company. Hatton was of little account, but his wife was the youngest of the Kembles, and she became almost a permanency in Manchester, with varying fortunes, as we shall see. Another newcomer was Wathen, who had become stagestruck after serving as a major in the army, and had been at Dublin under the assumed name of George. After his spell at Manchester he was at the Haymarket and Drury Lane, where he played comic servants and rustics with success. His first appearance at Manchester was in the same line, as Scrub in *The Beaux Stratagem*. T. Banks returned—no doubt to occupy the paint room on the departure of Dibdin.

During February Mrs. Crouch and Michael Kelly paid a visit of three nights, and in the following month Thomas King appeared as Ogleby and Falstaff. Apart from these special engagements the most interesting programme was for Mrs. Taylor's benefit on March 31, when *Coriolanus* and *The Winter's Tale* were performed. The first-named was played in Kemble's version, with Cooke in the title part and Mrs. Taylor as Volumnia. For Cooke's benefit a week later Jephson's tragedy, *The Duke of Braganza,* received its first Manchester performance. In the summer months Incledon and Bowden paid another visit, but of greater interest was the appearance of Munden, his first since the days of his stock company visits with Austin and Whitlock. In the meantime he had become the leading low comedian of the day, and one of his parts during the Manchester visit was Old Dornton in *The Road to Ruin,* a role he had created and since made famous. Of hardly less interest, Mrs. Siddons's son Henry, who, according to Tate Wilkinson looked amazingly like his Uncle John, accompanied Munden and performed Young Dornton.

Neither Cooke nor Mrs. Taylor was in the company

which opened a new season on December 1, 1794, and there were no new actors of note. To judge from the number of repeat performances, several productions were to the liking of the audience. One was Cumberland's new comedy, *The Jew*, in which Jabal was played by Barrett and Sheva by Ward. Sheridan's 'dramatic entertainment' called *The Camp* was another, and a third, *The Rage*, a comedy by Reynolds. Though not quoting any reference, Broadbent says 'in Manchester the comedy fell flat', but, as it was played five times during the regular season and was chosen as a benefit piece, this judgment seems at fault.

Evidently the weather was very severe that winter. At least two performances, on February 20 and 24 were cancelled because of it, and in the spring and summer there was some rioting owing to the scarcity of corn, resulting in an order made in July that all public-houses were to close by seven o'clock and that all persons out of doors after nine might be called upon to give an account of themselves.

On May 1, less than a week after his appearance as Dogberry, Barrett, the leading low comedy man for several seasons, died in Manchester. Throughout his engagement in the town he had lodged with a Mr. Cundell in Fountain Street, and for some years he had played at the Haymarket in the summer. The custom of placing addresses on benefit announcements enables us to follow the movements of players through the years and to indulge in some gentle speculation about them. For example, for some time past the Wards, the Banks and Mrs. Powell had all given 19, Falkner Street as their place of residence (all three ladies, it will be remembered, were sisters). In this summer, however, there is a parting. Banks has now set up house in Chatham Street, Piccadilly, and the Wards are at 5, George Street, which is now also the address of Mrs. Powell. One need not assume disagreement but rather growing importance and security.

Perhaps, indeed, as critics were never tired of pointing out, the managers were doing very well for themselves out of the theatre. We can only guess, of course, but it is one of several interesting queries raised by no more than a few printed addresses.

Another matter, not in the theatre, but definitely in the world of entertainment, was the visit to the Great Room, Bull's Head, at the end of April, of 'the Celebrated Chevaliere D'Eon' who promised to make 'A Great Assault D'Armes with an English Gentleman'. This went on for several nights and 'in case Ladies and Gentlemen shall have an inclination to dance' a 'Band of Military Music' would be in attendance. This colourful personality, after acting as agent for the French king in Russia and as diplomatic representative in London, was suspected of being a woman, and obtained a pension from the French government on the condition of wearing female clothes. The notices of the Manchester visit give full details of the Chevaliere's career, based on the assumption that they are writing about a woman. "She" was subsequently proved to be a man, but no doubt the appeal of a woman swordsman of such ability accounts for "her" highly successful tours through this country.

At the theatre Cunningham, from the Theatre Royal, Dublin, performed *Hamlet* on May 25, with Tyrrell as the King, Banks once more as the Ghost and Miss Daniels as Ophelia. Then John Palmer played a few nights and there was a visit from Mr. and Mrs. Pope. Between these two there was for three nights an entertainment called *The Thespian Panorama,* provided by Munden, Bowden and Rees, the last well-known at Covent Garden as a mimic. This seems to have been very much what we would now call a variety bill.

On October 29 Mrs. Shepley[59] had the use of the theatre for her benefit concert, for which she announced the engagement of Mr. Nield 'previous to his going to London'. She assured intending patrons that the theatre would be well aired. Nor must we overlook the exhibition at Salford Fair in November of 'The Spotted Indian Youth' described as 'The Most Astonishing and Wonderful Production of Human Nature ever seen in Europe'. As Sheffield was to have the privilege of seeing him, he could stay no longer than the period of the Fair. Mr. Handy, from the Royal Circus, London, was also free for only a few nights when he arrived at the New Circus in August, but he contrived to be in Manchester still some two months later.[60]

With the start of the 1795-6 season on November 25 we obtain another source of information. The *Monthly Mirror* began publication in London. It called itself a journal "Reflecting Men and Manners, with Strictures on their Epitome the Stage", and it gave news of various provincial theatres. Its Manchester correspondents changed with bewildering frequency, and sometimes two were reporting at the same period and overlapped. Neverthelesss they often provide facts otherwise lacking and with comments which show care and knowledge.

Prior to the opening, the managers had announced that tickets for the season were available at three and a half guineas, which admitted the purchaser 'to any part of the Theatre before the curtain'. There would be from forty-four to fifty performances. Transferable tickets would cost one guinea more.

The opening plays were *Douglas* and a comic opera, *The Adopted Child*. The newcomers were Eastmure from Bath and Glassington from Liverpool, and Hamerton was back again. In *Douglas* Tyrrell and Mrs. Ward were the principals, and in the other Master Daniels, junior, was the adopted child. Cumberland's *First Love* received its first local performance on December 4 and was repeated on December 16 and on January 6. An announcement by the managers in the *Mercury* for December 29 respectfully acquainted the public that 'from Complaints having been made of the coldness of the Pit they have caused a stove to be erected that answers every purpose to make it warm and comfortable'.

The correspondent of the *Monthly Mirror* was not so easily comforted. In the January number he makes a biting attack on the management: 'if this populous town evinced no more liberality in supporting the managers, than they do in entertaining the town, it would be much if they "got salt to their pottage"'. They are, he says, 'experiencing a considerable conditional abatement of rent' but evidently making poor use of it. He hopes Banks will find reinforcements, 'for in Ward, as a manager, no confidence is placed'. The scenery is shabby and threatens to collapse. Of the actors Hamerton's comedy is lifeless and inattentive and his tragedy little better; he is, indeed, 'a poor apology for the loss of the excellent and unfortunate Cooke'. Mrs. Ward has to play youthful and unsuitable parts 'for want of some youthful and subordinate actresses', and Ward himself 'is very agreeable'. In spite of disadvantages of voice, person and age, 'he possesses a portion of the true vis comica'. The critic was kindest to Swendall who 'never misunderstands his author, nor ever mixes the ridiculous with the humorous'.

That this critic was not alone in his dissatisfaction is indicated by an announcement of January 5, which informed the public that 'Constables will be placed about the Theatre to take into custody those who shall throw any thing into the Pit, on the Stage, into the Orchestra or any other Part of the Theatre'. On this day, Mrs. Coates began a special engagement which ended on January 11, when for her benefit were played *The Provok'd Husband* and *High Life Below Stairs*. There was soon further disorder in the theatre, this time about the playing of "God Save the King". *The Mercury,* of

March 8, ended a long account by noting that since the trouble it had been announced that "God Save the King" would be sung each night after the entertainment and that 'last Wednesday there was not the slightest disturbance'. The *Monthly Mirror* also had something to say of 'the violent dispute between a party of officers and others, on account of some imagined irreverence on the part of two or three persons, when "God Save the King" was demanded'. The officers, in his opinion, 'behaved shamefully ill, and one gentleman was dangerously hurt in the scuffle'. An action at law was likely.[61] In the same number, the critic thought poorly of Richard Wilson, who had just completed a special visit of six nights; but while repeating his former poor opinion of the company generally, he had some good words for Tyrrell; 'he is a performer of great merit, and a considerable favourite with the inhabitants'.

Had the critic but known it, help was at hand, for Cooke reappeared on March 15. His life was full of crises and calamities, mostly self-imposed, but none is more colourful than his joining the army after—or more probably during—a drunken bout, and being bought out by Ward and Banks and conveyed with great care back to Manchester. He opened in *The Man of the World* and later played King John, Mark Antony, and for his benefit on April 25 Giles Overreach in *A New Way to Pay Old Debts,* afterwards reciting Dryden's "Ode on St. Cecilia's Day". For the benefit of Miss Daniels, he recited Collins's "Ode on the Passions" and for Tyrrell, Gray's "Elegy". When Mr. and Mrs. Swendall chose *The Comedy of Errors* to follow *Oroonoko* it was stated to be the first local performance of Shakespeare's comedy. Connor, the former manager and now landlord of the Crown and Thistle, Old Church Yard, was given a benefit, and Cooke appeared as Hamlet to the Claudius of Tyrrell, the Polonius of Swendall and the Ophelia of Miss

Daniels. Connor himself, reappearing after seven years, was First Gravedigger.

At Whitsun Mrs. Siddons came for a season of six nights. Only four of her plays were announced: she played Isabella, Mrs. Beverley, Lady Percy and Lady Macbeth, supported by Cooke in each part. One must assume that the little advertising done by the managers on this visit is an indication of Mrs. Siddons's drawing power. Neither Ward nor Banks was willing to spend money without good reason.

The theatre was not opened again during the summer, but Handy had the Circus in full spate. Astley, it was announced, would receive £300 for twelve nights, but he stayed a further ten, and later there was Ducrow. Handy made a special announcement on September 27 that, 'Saturday next being Acres Fair Day', he would perform 'to give persons in the country the opportunity of seeing the Circus'. During August a Mr. Breslaw was at the Bull's Head with his 'New Invented Capital Deceptions and Experiments'. He was evidently successful, for an intended stay of two days stretched out to the end of the month.

After being closed for seven months, the theatre reopened on January 2, 1797. A few days earlier Cooke had married Miss Daniels at Chester, and they both were present on the opening night, when he played Hastings to Mrs. Ward's Jane Shore in the tragedy of that name and Mrs. Cooke was Eliza in the musical entertainment of *The Poor Sailor*. Important newcomers to the company were Mr. and Mrs. Andrew Cherry. She played Alicia in *Jane Shore,* but he did not appear until January 11, when he played Solus in *Every One has his Fault* and Lazarillo in *Two Strings to your Bow*. Cherry, who was to become one of the foremost comedians of his day, was an Irishman to whom Tate Wilkinson had given his first engagement in this country in 1792. 'My bonny, sensible, little Mr. Cherry from Dublin', Wilkinson calls him, and pays him high tribute: 'he has the peculiar excellence as a comedian, that when he has to perform a character not so suited to his genius and abilities, yet still it is not Cherry, but the character so justly conceived, that you perceive the skill of the artist perhaps more when he is out of his walk, than when in'.[62]

The *Monthly Mirror* had a long account of these early performances. Cooke's Sir Pertinax 'is allowed by all to be a diamond of the first water; even Glassington's Lord Lambercourt cannot spoil the effect of it. Hamerton ranted Egerton as usual'. In *The Earl of Warwick* Mrs. Ward and Cooke were excellent, and 'Eastmure's Dicky Gossip showed he could be diverting when his buffoonery will let him'. He thought Banks a Wronghead for playing that part in *The Provok'd Husband*, but he turns again to praise Cooke as Sir Archy, finding his Scottish accent natural, whereas Macklin's was not. He speaks of Cherry's 'comic phiz and voice' but thinks the latter has acquired a sameness through playing old man parts. On the whole, however, 'he is the best we have had in his way since Munden'. The critic is not impressed by the success at Shrewsbury and Chester of Miss Ward, daughter of the manager. She has improved 'in nothing but confidence'. The scenery, newly painted, comes in for tart comment, particularly the figure of Britannia who 'has been, during the late touching up, metamorphosed into a modern lady. Her head has been, to speak in aldermanic phrase, turbaned, and her whole dress is now quite the rage. One side of her bosom is covered with muslin, the remainder is left in a state of nature'. In its present 'pale-fac'd daub', he concludes, 'it is neither more nor less than a preposterous indecency'. He notes further that the boxes, not before they needed it, have been newly lined, and there are festoons of scarlet and gold on the front of the lower ones and blue and gold on the higher.[63]

In the next number of the *Monthly Mirror* the same critic takes up the story again. Cooke's Richard III exhibited him to great advantage; 'What indeed does not?' In the same play Banks and Turpin had to be prompted throughout, but there was no hissing. 'We are not too free with our plaudits but we never hiss'. He makes fun of Ward's unnecessary sprightliness in *The Way to get Married* and suggests if he could become a little rheumatic without being lame, he would be the best provincial Lewis in England.

On January 30 Miss Allingham, said to be a former resident of Manchester, and sister of the dramatist, John Till Allingham, began a special engagement, in the course of which she played Juliet, Rosalind, Hermione and Beatrice, ending with what the *Monthly Mirror* called 'a bumper benefit' as Belvidera and Roxalana. The same critic praised her performances, but thought her unlucky, in that she was outshone by Cooke throughout her visit. Mrs. Ward is soundly chastised for not appearing with Miss Allingham; if it is pride which keeps her away when visiting actors are playing, it is discourteous to them and to the audience. Banks, the critic points out, behaves quite differently; moreover, now that he has become corpulent, he leaves hero parts to others and plays old men—an obvious blow in Mrs. Ward's direction. He cannot forgo his customary taunt at Hamerton, though he says as his ranting increases, so does his popularity with the Monday gallery. Turpin 'promises to be a pleasant singer and tolerable performer', but he has no use for Rawlings, another newcomer. He finds a present tendency towards cutting well-known plays, as for instance omitting Sir Fretful from *The Critic*. A final indiscreet comment about Cooke's domestic affairs is hastily withdrawn in the next number.

When *The Merchant of Venice* was performed on February 14 with Cooke as Shylock, not only was Mrs. Ward the Portia, but Banks refuted the *Monthly Mirror* by playing Bassanio. *The Iron Chest* by the younger Colman had its first local performance on March 9 with, wrote our critic, very little music. 'It is strange' he continued, 'that such pieces should be got up without good choruses, and in Lancashire too'. Two other plays, *A Cure for the Heart Ache* and *Wives as they Were* 'have been successful, of course'.

For Cherry's benefit on March 22 the comedian brought out a comic opera of his own, *The Outcasts*, with music by Moorhead, leader of the theatre orchestra. The *Monthly Mirror*, which preferred to call it a farce, thought it poor stuff, but had a good word for Miss Cherry, 'who cannot have been more than eleven' but spoke and acted admirably. Cherry also gave "A Comic Dissertation on Hobby Horses" for Hamerton's benefit. A patriotic novelty, *Cape St. Vincent*, formed the afterpiece at the joint benefit of Rawlings and Glassington, all the illuminations 'having been brought from London at considerable expense'. Another joint benefit was for Turpin and Moorhead, which included a comic song "The Muffin Man" composed by Moorhead and sung by Cherry. Moorhead also included for the first time his overture "Alonzo and Imogine".

The company departed for Chester to perform during the races, but were back on May 8, when H. E. Johnston began a special engagement of four nights. Then there was a benefit for Clough, who combined the duties of double-bass player with those of landlord of the George and Dragon. Mrs. Siddons had been announced to appear on May 29 for four nights, but she arrived in time to start three nights earlier in *Jane Shore,* with Cooke as Hastings and Tyrrell as Belmour. On the following Monday, Tuesday and Wednesday she was seen as Athanais in *Theodosius*, Zara in *The Mourning Bride* and Isabella in *Measure for Measure*, announced as the first Manchester performance, with Cooke as the Duke. Mrs. Siddons played an extra night on June 6, when *Theodosius* was repeated. These performances virtually brought the season to a close, and gain extra significance from the fact that Cooke's career as a stock actor in Manchester also closed. He was to return, of course, for special visits after his acceptance in London.

Ward and Banks returned from their seasons at Shrewsbury and Chester to make a fresh start on Boxing Day, 1797. They were without Cooke, and Hamerton, Eastmure and Mrs. Cooke had also gone, but the managers more than made up the loss in numbers, for Egan (from Edinburgh), Fisher (from Bath), and Blandford were present when the season started and Raymond, from Dublin, soon followed. There was also Miss Smyth, and Mrs. Hatton returned and Connor came out of retirement. George Raymond, who is best remembered as the biographer of R. W. Elliston, seems to have made a considerable impression during his stay in Manchester. *The Dramatic Mirror* (1808) speaks of his 'majestic figure and flexible features' and praises him in characters 'which call forth the stronger passions'.

The opening pieces were *The Way to get Married* and *Peeping Tom* and on January 9 *She Stoops to Conquer* was revived, with Egan as Marlow, Cherry as Tony and Mrs. Cherry as Kate. A fourth member of the family, Miss F. Cherry, appeared for the first time a fortnight later. Raymond, described by the *Monthly Mirror* as 'a fine, tall figure, though somewhat heavy in appearance',[64] then arrived and shared the leads with Egan. Another newcomer, Mrs. Bernard, was seen as Widow Brady in the ever-popular *The Irish Widow*. Two new comedies were given and repeated several times: Reynolds's *The Will* and Colman's *The Heir at Law,* Raymond being Dick Dowlas in the latter piece.

At this point "Monk" Lewis, the novelist who wrote Gothic romances, those forerunners of the modern thriller, came prominently into the programmes. *Raymond and Agnes*, described as a 'Grand Serious Pantomime' was 'founded chiefly on the principal episode in the Romance of the Monk'. It had music by Reeve and new scenery and machinery. But the real sensation was clearly Lewis's play, *The Castle Spectre*. There is no contemporary account of its reception, but as its second performance was on March 13 and its seventh and last on March 21, everything must have been pushed on one side to meet popular demand. Raymond played Osmond and Mrs. Bernard, the Spectre.

Immediately before this, on March 2, it had been announced that the proceeds from the performance on that night would be given to 'The Voluntary Contribution for the Defence of our Country'. On March 6 the *Mercury* gave figures. The takings had been £43 19*s*., but there was added a list of donations, which included £10 from each of the managers, £5 from the band of the Theatre Royal, and a guinea or half-a-guinea from most of the performers.

When the benefits started, the afterpiece for that of Mrs. Powell, *The Raft*, included 'the manner of forging and preparing red hot balls; with the destruction and burning of the French Rafts, for their proposed Invasion of England'. Tyrrell struck the right tone for the moment by reviving *Henry V* and Raymond chose a play not before seen in Manchester, *The Stranger*, in which Ward played the title part, Raymond was Baron Stanfort, Cherry was Peter, and Mrs. Bernard, Mrs. Haller.

The summer brought an unusual number of special engagements, and incidentally the renewal of reports in the *Monthly Mirror*. Mrs. Second, a well-known vocalist, included Rosina in her performances, and then Samuel Ryley appeared, giving among other things his one-man entertainment, *New Brooms*. For Race Week there was an extra attraction, when J. P. Kemble appeared as Hamlet and

Richard III, and for his benefit on June 6 the Stranger in the play of that name, which he had played at its first performance in London. After Kemble came W. T. Lewis, later to be well-known as the Liverpool manager, and in turn he was followed by Jack Bannister, making his first appearance in Manchester. The next visitors were Charles Incledon, the most famous of all stage vocalists in this period, and Miss Leak, who sang the principal parts in *Lionel and Clarissa*, with Cherry as Colonel Oldboy and Ward as Jessamy. These various engagements gave rise to a conflict of opinion in the *Monthly Mirror*, not as to the merit of the performances but to Manchester's reception and support of her visitors. A critic in the July issue, after stating that the town had experienced a dramatic surfeit, the company having been performing nearly six months together, went on to claim that Bannister, Lewis and Kemble had not received the attention due to their merits, and that Incledon and Miss Leak had also performed with the same ill-success. He was taken to task 'for the honour of Manchester' by another critic, who was able to quote figures to support his protest. Kemble's benefit was £97, 'here a great receipt', Bannister had £100 12s. and Incledon £115 11s., the latter 'a greater sum than has been received at these doors for many years'. Lewis 'a most excellent actor' was less fortunate, but all were warmly received.

Beginning on September 1 Michael Kelly and Mrs. Crouch played a brief season of musical pieces.

When the new season opened, the profits on December 5 were given 'toward the relief of the widows and orphans of the brave fellows who suffered in the glorious action commanded by the gallant Admiral Lord Nelson'. *The School for Scandal* was performed, with Penson, a newcomer from York, as Sir Peter Teazle. Penson had been engaged to fill the place left by Cherry's departure to Bath.[65]

Grist also returned once more, but otherwise the company showed little change. On December 7, however, an actor later to become famous, Charles Mayne Young, appeared for the first time in Manchester as Douglas to the Lady Randolph of Mrs. Ward. Young, who was not yet twenty-two, had made his stage debut at Liverpool three months before under the assumed name of Green and had met with considerable success. His stay in Manchester was intended to be brief, but after equal success, as the *Monthly Mirror* noted, in Hamlet, Young Bevil and Romeo, he became a regular member of the company.

On Boxing Day a play well known to all lovers of Jane Austen, Mrs. Inchbald's *Lovers' Vows*, was performed for the first time in Manchester, with Young as Anhalt, Raymond as the Baron, and Penson as Verdun. Penson had already become a favourite. True to the tradition of serving heavy fare on New Year's Day, Otway's *The Orphan* was given, in which Young played Chamont. Young in a very short time was playing most of the leads, but unfortunately there is no local comment on his performances. At his debut at Liverpool the *Monthly Mirror* had devoted a long account to him, describing him as being evidently possessed of great feeling and sensibility, with expressive features and a voice finely toned, powerful and flexible. His person was described as 'well formed and elegant' and the writer pronounced with confidence that if he devoted himself to the stage, he would speedily place himself in the very first rank of actors. The speed with which he established himself in Manchester suggests that opinion there was in agreement with the Liverpool critic.

When *The Stranger* was revived on February 1 Raymond took the title part, and on February 12 Young played Romeo to the far from youthful Juliet of Mrs. Ward. The company was destitute of young leading ladies and throughout the season Mrs. Ward was to be seen in parts such as Imogen and Lady Teazle. She again played the lead with Young when Thomson's *Edward and Eleanora* was revived on March 25. On the same programme there was the 'Grand Spectacle' of *Blue Beard* as played at Drury Lane. The Band of the Cornwall Fencibles added to the entertainment. We have mentioned Mrs. Ward as Imogen, which she played for her benefit, to the Posthumus of Young, with Raymond as Iachimo, Ward as Cloten and Egan as Pisanio. There was nothing of special note during Whit week, but a reference to Young in the *Mercury* of May 21 may be noted. He had promised to appear at a benefit for Connor and Hill after which 'he positively takes his departure from our stage, where it is barely justice to say his reception has been as flattering to himself as his general performance has been pleasing to the town'.

The summer brought another large crop of special engagements. First were Incledon, Munden and Mrs. Atkins, the latter a singer who had graduated from Bath to the Haymarket and was the daughter of Mrs. Warrall, already noted as a former performer in Manchester. Jack Bannister returned once more, and in August Charles Dibdin the younger and his wife brought a company to play pieces of a very miscellaneous character, some of his own composition.[66] In the company was John Ducrow, who announced his benefit in the *Mercury* in very glowing terms, promising to 'go through those wonderful leaps from the Trampoline in particular one over Eighteen Grenadiers, with shouldered firelocks and fixed bayonets; also through a hogshead of Real Fire, and will fly over a grand Pyramid of Light'. Young Dibdin, for his benefit, produced an outsize playbill in which he made a long rhyming announcement of his plans. Before the new season began there was a notable concert at which the principal performers were Madame Mara, the great soprano, Bartleman the violinist, and Dragonetti, one of the greatest of double-bass players. Finally Samuel Ryley 'with a most grateful remembrance of past favours, intrudes himself once more on the public'. He gave *New Brooms* and a new pantomime he had composed for the occasion, in which the last scene represented the old Fair in an uproar.

The new season opened on December 16, 1799, with revivals of *The Castle Spectre* and *Rosina*. Three newcomers, Grant, Rowswall and Cross, were in the first piece and Miss Griffiths, destined to be a great favourite in Manchester in the following years, appeared as Rosina. The first performance of real interest was in February, when Sheridan's latest success, *Pizarro,* was given in Manchester for the first time. Rolla was played by Young, who was back again despite the apparently final farewell given him in the *Mercury,* Cross played Alonzo, and Egan, Grist, Grant, Rowswall, Miss Griffiths, and Mrs. Ward were also in the cast. The *Mercury,* which rarely contained any notices of performances at this period, made an exception in its favour; finding it performed

> in a very superior manner. The scenery is superb, the dresses characteristically elegant, the processions and music conducted with the utmost precision and correctness; and the performers in general, particularly Mr. Young and Mrs. Ward, exerted their talents to the greatest effect. Every praise and encouragement is due to the managers for their spirited and liberal conduct in bringing forth so magnificent a performance.

Another new play destined to become a stock favourite far and wide was *Speed the Plough* which Mrs. Ward announced for her benefit, although it had been produced at Covent Garden less than two months earlier.

Despite these outstanding items, all was not well. It was not merely that an outbreak of pamphleteering had begun, notably in a publication called *A Peep into the Theatre*

Royal, which the *Monthly Mirror* not unfairly dismissed as 'vulgar and scurrilous'; the *Monthly Mirror* critic himself, in the issue for March, 1800, makes it clear that there are grounds for discontent. The theatre, he tells us, had been very thinly attended. 'The town is dissatisfied with the company, which is by no means equal to what Manchester has been accustomed to, though we observe several names of respectability among the performers—Ward and Banks (the Managers), Young, Grist, Turpin, Penson, Mrs. Hatton, Mrs. Ward, Miss Griffiths, etc.'. He goes on to say that Raymond, now at Drury Lane, was a considerable favourite, both as an actor and a private character, and his loss was much regretted. Ward made a pathetic appeal on April 14 in the *Mercury*, stating that illness had kept him from his professional duties and this fact, coupled with the malignity of the pamphleteer attempting to poison the public mind against him, gave him little hope of profiting from taking a benefit. Nevertheless, 'he submits his situation to the public whom he has ever found his friend and patrons'. Unfortunately we do not know how the public reacted to this subtle approach.

Before Whit, George Davies Harley came from Dublin for an engagement of three nights, during which he played Richard III, Shylock, and Iago. There was nothing of unusual interest during Race Week. It was then announced that John Banks had decided to retire from management, and that his place as Ward's partner would be taken by Thomas Ludford Bellamy, who was the son of Richard Bellamy, Vicar-choral of St. Paul's Cathedral. The new manager had sung as a boy at subscription concerts in London, and later in oratorio. He then went to Ireland, but at the time of going to Manchester he had been on the professional stage only about three years. His wife was the daughter of Thomas Grist.

IV

1800—1807

THE NEW partnership of Ward and Bellamy redecorated the theatre before opening their season on December 3, 1800, with *The Wonder* and *Lock and Key*, half the receipts of the first night being given to the support of the soup shops established the previous year for the relief of the poor. Throughout this season the *Monthly Mirror* devoted a lot of space to Manchester, and we shall use it largely for a general view of events. In January the critic admitted that when the season opened the company was weak, 'but the managers have so recruited it as to render it one of the most respectable provincial companies in the Kingdom'. Bellamy 'certainly yields the palm to no stage singer, Incledon excepted', and Gordon, from Sheffield, was an admirable performer in the line of Bannister and Fawcett, 'with much original whim and sound judgment'. Excellent comedian though Penson was, he had shown himself this season 'rather too fond of grimace and gallery clap-trap'. Bengough declaimed well, but his acting lacked grace. In addition there were Turner, from Bath, Grist, D'Arcy, Stuart, Curtis and Swendall, the latter, 'always respectable because always chaste'. Mrs. Ward was so well known that no words of the critic could add to her fame; Mrs. Bellamy looked, on the evidence of her Amanthis and Angela, of superior merit; Mrs. Forbes was a 'pleasing Hoyden', and Mrs. D'Arcy a 'second-rate singer, with taste and some science'. Miss Griffiths had returned greatly improved in person, manner and voice and was already a great favourite. There were also Mrs. Bernard, Mrs. Swendall and Mrs. Bengough. 'For operas and musical farces', the critic continued, 'I think we may challenge any theatre in Great Britain; indeed a late representation of *Lionel and Clarissa* would not have disgraced the boards of Covent Garden'. This critic, who called himself 'Lover of the Drama' was supported by another in the same issue writing as 'Attentive Observer', who admits he has formerly been critical of the managers, but can now praise them. He agreed with his colleague at all points, and mentions that two more newcomers to the company are expected soon.

A third critic, calling himself 'Fidelis' makes his bow in the February number, and reported that Bellamy and Miss Griffiths 'are rising in favour, and their vocal abilities have introduced them to the concert room'. Rosalind, as played by Mrs. Bellamy 'was exquisite'. In March, 'J.C.O.' took up the tale, praising Lovegrove and another newcomer, Faulkner; finding Mrs. Bellamy unrivalled in sentimental parts 'but the same cannot be said of her romps'. He notes that Penson has followed the critics' advice and mended his ways.

'Fidelis' returns in April, carefully analyses Faulkner's merits and faults, and recommends him 'to assume a loftier deportment—to hold up his head and to tread the stage with more becoming dignity'. He makes a special point of praising Bengough, 'a promising young performer whose Pizarro, Glenalvon, Sir Philip Blandford and Iachimo are sustained very creditably'. Bengough had started with inferior parts and by merit had won through to better ones. This critic has nothing good to say of Turner, but he is ready to praise Mrs. Bellamy in everything and cannot understand 'J.C.O.'s objection to her romps.

'Dramaticus', another of the seemingly inexhaustible list

of *Monthly Mirror* correspondents, has some interesting things to say of benefits in the May number. 'When it is considered that performers in general are nearly as much influenced, in making their engagements, by the probability or improbability of productive benefits, as by the salaries offered, it will quickly be perceived how much more easily theatrical skill can be procured for a place where it is *voluntarily* rewarded, as well as discovered, than when only the latter part of the business is done'. If the public think a player deserving, the matter is in their own hands, and it should not be necessary to solicit and flatter them. He then gives a list of the recent benefits: Gordon £115; Miss Griffiths £110; Mrs. Ward £109; Penson £102; Connor £100; Mrs. Bellamy £99; Miss Ward £90; Grist £85; Bellamy £80; Bengough £77; Ward £75; Turner £75; the D'Arcys £65; the Swendalls £55 and Faulkner £25. Allowing that Faulkner did not come until the season was well on its way, he had played leading parts and his public reward suggests a lower estimate of him than that of the critics quoted.

Mrs. Siddons's visit in May seems to have passed unnoticed by the *Monthly Mirror,* but the balance was restored with a glowing account of Cooke's reappearance in August, when he was accompanied by Mr. and Mrs. Pope. The critic —this time unnamed—began in lyrical fashion: 'At length, his "brow crown'd with victorious wreaths" came our long-expected favourite, Cooke, to revisit his Manchester friends'. The 'loud and general plaudits which greeted him on his entrance appeared so many congratulations on his success in "a happier clime".' The Popes gave him fine support; the rest of the company, we are bitingly told, comprised 'part of the performers of last season and a few miserable strollers, apparently swept from neighbouring barns'. The engagement was an unusually strenuous one, for eleven consecutive nights were played, with only Sunday rest. Cooke performed most of his favourite parts: Richard III, Othello, Shylock, Stukely, Sir Archy, Hamlet, Sir Pertinax and Macbeth. The critic has an interesting comment to make on his portrayal of Stukely in *The Gamester*: 'We are not merely regarding with animation a change of features, but with astonishment are exploring the inmost recesses of the heart'. The Popes' benefit produced £92 and Cooke's £110, when he played Macbeth.

Before the next season started on December 6, 1801, the theatre was again redecorated, 'very elegantly' according to the *Monthly Mirror*, and as the country was at peace an address 'by a Gentleman of Manchester' was spoken by Ward on the first three nights, which pointed out that 'the Peace was so favourable to the manufacturers of the place'. Several of the former company had gone, notably Lovegrove, Leonard, Turner, Miss Griffiths and Mrs. Forbes. Newcomers included Huddart from Dublin, Carr, and Mrs. Addison, a talented singer who replaced Miss Griffiths.

On the opening night, *The Belle's Stratagem* and *The Wedding Day* were given, and for New Year's Day *George Barnwell* was allowed to put across its heavy moral. Apart from the actors mentioned, Hollingsworth, an old favourite, had returned to the company. At the end of January John Quick paid a short visit. Later productions included a revival of *Speed the Plough* by desire of the Agricultural Society, during the second act of which was introduced 'an exact representation of the Ploughing Match held this day at Withington'. A novelty of a different kind was the two performances of *Pizarro*; on the first night Faulkner played Rolla and Huddart Alonzo; on the second the roles were reversed.

The *Monthly Mirror* had less to say about this season, though two critics 'Amicus' and 'A Plain Dealer' shared the responsibility and were by no means always in agreement. Both praised Huddart, 'Amicus' finding that he possessed 'great advantages of voice, figure and expression of countenance'. Though by no means inelegant, he could do with a little more firmness and majesty of deportment. The critics were poles apart on Carr. To the 'Plain Dealer' he was 'destitute of merit'; to his colleague versatile and correct in judgment. 'Amicus' writes of Hollingsworth's 'rich, comic vein of natural and unforced humour—highly relished in Manchester' and he highly commended Penson as Caleb Quotem: 'scarcely inferior to Fawcett, and somewhat more chaste'. 'A Plain Dealer' commended Swendall and remarked that 'Mrs. Addison's musical abilities are of the first rate; she may be said to serve three masters, as she also takes the lead in Manchester and Liverpool concerts'.

Cooke paid another visit in June, and Incledon in August. A less distinguished visitor was Mrs. Clutterbuck, who recited and sang. At a concert in the theatre on October 19 Madame Dussek, well-known both as vocalist and instrumentalist, appeared under the direction of Tainewiez.

Bellamy was given a stormy reception when the new season opened on December 1, 1802. The discontent arose from his having left the company before the end of the previous season, and his appearance caused such tumult that Bellamy obtained permission to proceed with his performance only by promising, if allowed to finish the evening, he would never appear on that stage again. Needless to say, feelings did not remain at this pitch and his threat—or promise—was not put into effect. Disturbances of this kind were common enough in the theatres everywhere at this time; the players were reminded in no uncertain terms that they were servants of the public. It was perhaps particularly apparent in an area growing as rapidly as Manchester, both in numbers and industrial importance. Political self-consciousness was rising, frustrated and therefore likely to be made more eruptive by the lack of representation in Parliament, and its expression was likely to be given utterance anywhere in public assemblies such as the theatre. Although there is so much we do not know about the theatre of this period (and consequently opinion should be put forward with caution) one gets the impression that what had changed was less the standard at the theatre than the temper of the public, and its desire to exhibit a growing sense of power. This should be borne in mind, and set alongside the obvious fact that the theatre was now too small for its purpose.

After reporting the tumult mentioned above, the *Monthly Mirror*, for whom a critic under the name 'Mancuniensis' had now appeared, expressed the opinion that the new company was an excellent one. Richardson, back after an absence of eight years, was much improved, Cross received commendation, and 'Mills, I think, is one of the most promising actors on the English stage'. Another critic, 'X', praised the scene painting of Coyle, 'whose pieces would do credit to the boards of the metropolis'. Huddart was making rapid progress in the public esteem. In *A Tale of Mystery* his Romaldi was excellent and 'in the last scene he is terrific to sublimity'. His Stranger, Rolla, and Othello were admired as performances rarely equalled and 'his manner strikes us as truly original'. Mills has also impressed this critic, and of Gordon he writes 'his humour never fails to please the gods of the gallery, nor his good person to secure the admiration of the ladies in the boxes'. He notes that two recent comedies have been loudly condemned, 'the town of Manchester having lately assumed the prerogative of a London audience'. A third article, by 'Candid', although confirming his colleague's opinions of Huddart and insisting on the claims of Mrs. Hatton as a vocalist, is at a loss to understand the public attitude to this lady: 'they allow the excellence of this actress in hoydens and chambermaids, but refuse to honour her benefit with their presence, because, forsooth, they approve not of the effrontery that is necessarily attached to those characters'. But 'Candid' is not at all satisfied with the management; receipts, he says, were never so good, yet the managers do not give the public plays which are to be found in the advertisements of Mr. M'Cready at Bolton. Even the operas are not decently performed and there is no adequate replacement for Miss Griffiths or Mrs. Addison. Gordon is accused of 'judicious deviations from the text'. The ear is stunned in almost every sentence by his favourite expressions: 'My dear fellor' and 'My dear soul'.

Apart from the performers mentioned above, newcomers this season included Scriven, from Newcastle, who played Tony Lumpkin, and Simms. There was *George Barnwell* again on New Year's Day, and in March, Huddart played Hamlet to the Ghost of Richardson, with Swendall as Polonius, Penson as First Gravedigger and Mrs. Mills as Ophelia. A performance of *The Rivals*, for the benefit of 'the intended House of Recovery', had Bengough as Captain Absolute, Mrs. Bellamy as Julia, Penson as Sir Anthony, Huddart as Falkland, Ward as Rob Acres and Mrs. Tayleure as Mrs. Malaprop. The last named was the former Mrs. Bernard, who had married a member of the theatre orchestra.[67]

When the company returned from Chester in May,[68] one of the attractions was a new pantomime called *Preston Guild*. Coyle had been busy, his views of local scenes having been 'taken on the spot'. They included 'Getty's Royal Oak, Manchester'; 'The Crescent, Salford'; various views of Preston; and 'an exact representation of the procession of the different corporated trades taken on the spot by Mr. Coyle'.

After summer visits from Cooke and Incledon which had by this time become annual events, the new season began on

December 2, 1803, with a performance 'for the benefit of the Patriotic Fund', which produced £124. The pieces were *Pizarro* and a musical entertainment, *Little Bob and Little Ben*, and all went well until, between the pieces, Ward came forward to speak "An Address to the Patriotism of the British Nation". 'I am very sorry to say', reports the *Monthly Mirror*, 'strong marks of disapprobation were shewn and he was prevented from speaking by loud hisses, and, at last, but not without difficulty, he obtained permission to proceed'. It is well to note that this occurred before the first appearance of *The Townsman* on December 7. This publication, the work of a local eccentric, James Watson, who kept a druggist's shop and was known as 'the Doctor', came out weekly at first but later at irregular intervals, the profits being stated to be for the Patriotic Fund. The price was increased from one penny to two after the first number. To quote the *Monthly Mirror*, it 'threatened destruction and annihilation to the managers, and their adherents, for not furnishing them with a better company, or, in short, such a one as they could approve of. But what kind of a corps must that be? For the fickleness of those individuals is such, that the performers of the two London houses, jointly, could not satisfy them for more than a season'. The critic makes it plain that only a trifling part of the town shares the view of *The Townsman*, since 'the present company is certainly as respectable as any out of the metropolis', but the publication clearly provided ammunition for the small section determined to cause trouble for any reason that might be to hand, and for some nights there was 'a tumult of uproar and confusion'. Nevertheless, as the critic went on to suggest, 'the houses this season have been too productive to suppose the public at large could have been influenced by this scurrilous publication, yet, strange to say, several of the actors who have been most liberally applauded on the stage, have been lashed most unmercifully by the *Townsman* on the following Saturday'.[69]

The conflict went on through the season. It produced a pamphlet, *An Appeal to the Town*, from a minor actor, White, one of those assailed by *The Townsman*, and the writer of the latter journal himself wrote to the *Monthly Mirror* spreading much heat but little light, but insisting that he was defending the freedom of the Press, which the thespian despots were determined to suppress unless it contained nothing but flattery of themselves. He further protested that he was not leading the feelings of the public but only expressing feelings which already existed. And he accused the aforesaid White of having written what he regarded as abusive things about his paper in the *Monthly Mirror*. And so it went on, but at least the *Monthly Mirror* gave figures for benefit receipts at the end of the season, which provides less controversial material and in its way throws useful light on the situation. There were three special engagements, Cooper £95, C. M. Young £60 18s. and Stephen Kemble £73 15s. The members' benefits were: Mrs. Ward £137; Miss Ward £129; Bengough and Penson, each £115; Huddart £112; Miss Jackson £111; Mrs. Bellamy £107; Worrall (Pit-office Keeper) £105;[70] Corrinor (Box Book-Keeper) £97; Gordon £95; Richardson £90; Swendall £79: Mr. and Mrs. Mills £79; and so on through several other names to Mrs. Hatton, joint bottom of the list with £41, bearing out what the critic had said. These figures are of interest, not merely because the amounts generally are higher than in earlier years, but also because the Wards are out on top, and Mrs. Bellamy also high. It will be noted, however, that neither manager took a personal benefit. Mrs. Hatton was granted a further joint benefit at the end of the season, but the receipts are not known.

The dust of battle having settled, a note can be made of other events during that season. Thomas Abthorpe Cooper, whose visit was listed in the benefits already mentioned, was usually announced as an American actor, though in fact he was born in London. He appeared in both countries with very varied results, his best period being in the winter before his Manchester visit, when he played a series of leading parts at Drury Lane. Of the other special visitors mentioned among the benefits, Young was a member of the Liverpool company and Stephen Kemble a manager in the North-East. On March 6, 'a new grand Allegorical Pantomimic Spectacle' was performed, called *Cinderella, or the Little Glass Slipper*. This had been given at Drury Lane on January 3 and is of special interest as marking the start of that most popular of all pantomime subjects. In March also a new comedy by Andrew Cherry, *The Soldier's Daughter*, was first seen in Manchester, with a cast including Swendall, Huddart, Penson, Mrs. and Miss Ward. We have already noted Mrs. Ward's record benefit. There was a special reason for it (not noted by the critic) for the Duke of Gloucester was present and the performance was 'by his Command'. Cherry's play already mentioned was chosen for this occasion, no doubt being thought appropriate, since the Duke's visit was primarily to review the Manchester Volunteers on Sale Moor.

The next season began in sensational style on November 12, 1804, for Master Betty appeared, and in Manchester as everywhere else, filled the theatre and was the subject of conversation throughout the town. Opinion will always be divided on the merits of this boy, and there must always be something absurd and incongruous in his attempting the classic tragic roles. People who ought to have known better lost their heads about him and made outrageous claims. That he had astonishing talent can hardly be denied, and the public, then as always, was ready to be entertained by the latest novelty. Some indication of the excitement his coming caused is contained in an incident printed by the *Mercury,* that 'a gentleman who possessed eight Box Tickets for Monday has refused an offer of sixteen guineas for them'. Betty opened in *Lovers' Vows* and followed with Young Norval, Octavian (in *The Mountaineers*) Tancred, Hamlet, and, for his benefit, Achmet. The receipts of these performances tell their own tale. The highest was £169, the lowest £122. For Betty's benefit the prices were doubled and £300 was the result. Including this, the young actor was said to have left Manchester £600 better off than when he arrived.[71]

An epidemic of alleged infant prodigies followed this success. The eight years old Master Benwell was followed by eleven years old Miss Quantrell, who played Young Norval and 'went through the Broad Sword exercises in the character of a Female Volunteer'. Less than a month later one Master Frederick Brown, also eleven years old, and announced as 'the Celebrated Ormskirk Roscius', challenged Betty on his own ground by playing Frederick in *Lovers' Vows*. Each of these was mildly praised in the *Mercury,* but the craze soon died.

The start of the regular season, after the departure of Betty, had been marked by more heckling of the managers. Mr. Ward was hissed on his first appearance, and on his asking what the ladies and gentlemen 'were pleased to want' was told 'A better company for Manchester'. He assured them he had travelled nearly seven hundred miles in search of performers, and better than his present company were not to be found. This produced only laughter, but the play proceeded, though but little that Ward said could be heard. Bellamy was later similarly assailed. He was asked why actors such as Miss Griffiths and Young were not engaged. Bellamy turned the argument on the audience by asserting 'that the benefits would not bring any first-rate performer to Manchester; salary to the performer was no object; if he could be insured a good benefit, he would come without salary'. The *Monthly Mirror* commented 'this, though a little wonderful, was suffered to pass, on being followed by a promise to engage and bring to Manchester several first-rate performers, if possible. Since when, we have neither seen nor heard of them—so much for promises'.

How far this dissatisfaction represented the general feeling of the town, it is difficult to say. It was asserted that the managers were making plenty of money by paying small salaries and relying on the benefits to satisfy the actors, as Bellamy's excuse seems to admit. But, the argument went on, the theatre was not big enough to produce benefits that were really tempting. On the other hand, the company had now remained substantially unchanged for a number of years, which suggests that the actors were satisfied they could not do better elsewhere, and that they continued to receive the support of the town—a view strengthened by the rise in benefit receipts, several in this season amounting to £140, which would have seemed an impossible figure only a few years before. It may have been, of course, that some section of the audience wanted any change rather than none, but more likely the general temper was a mixture of the growing—and probably inflated—sense of Manchester's importance, and the very real feeling, increasingly shared both behind and before the curtain, that a larger theatre must come soon.

The *Monthly Mirror* published a long review of the season, in general summing up that 'our theatricals have had a very successful run' and the benefits good on the whole. Bannister and Miss De Camp had been the first special visitors, then Mrs. Mountain, whose support had been poor. Nor did Johnstone and Cherry have the expected welcome, though hot weather, which made the theatre uncomfortable, had something to do with this. But there was another reason, which throws an interesting light on the general situation.

The rumour had gone out that Cherry was to return to the company for the following season to the exclusion of Penson, this 'apprehension' causing him to have 'very little applause for his exertions'. To close the special engagements, Cooke had returned once more.

Reviewing the individual performers, Ward, in Lewis's cast of characters, 'is very great; he is always pleasing, as a performer, but very seldom seen'—a circumstance not entirely attributable to the gout. Huddart and Swendall are highly praised, and Bellamy's singing is commended but 'owing to an uncommon irritability of temper' he was not on good terms with the town. The critic announced that he had sold his share to Ward, and was starting up in management in Ireland, with Gordon as his partner. This meant the loss of Mrs. Bellamy also, and it was rumoured that other players were going. Gordon had been a great favourite, and so was Penson, not equalled out of London. Bengough had been kept busy playing parts of all kinds, and although not devoid of faults, he was much liked. The critic goes through the list, finding more to approve than to blame; ending with the dancers, of whom Bland was a good harlequin and Cipriani an excellent clown.

The ladies were then discussed, with high praise for Mrs. Ward and Mrs. Bellamy. The latter's loss to the company 'will be almost irreparable'. Her figure on the stage was beautiful and 'according to the present rules of the management, no performer of equal merit could be procured for double the largest salary given'. The critic regrets that Miss Ward, 'like her sire, is so seldom seen', but he puts in a good word once more for Mrs. Hatton, who is 'of great value to the company'. But Miss Jackson again receives no support; from the critic, that is, for despite the criticism of her implied in public clamour for Miss Griffiths, her benefit receipts suggest that she had a considerable following. The critic ends his summary by announcing that Young is likely to share the management next season; 'and it is sincerely wished he may have more authority respecting the business of the theatre than Mr. Bellamy had, otherwise we shall be little bettered by his coming'. As a final word, he tells us that a new theatre is spoken of, but not yet begun.

Master Betty again appeared in Manchester in advance of the regular season, and played ten nights commencing with November 18, 1805. The *Monthly Mirror,* still relying on 'A Constant Reader' for its information, reported that Betty was well received, though with less enthusiasm than on his first visit. This, the critic thought, was 'not from any falling off of his abilities, which are certainly, on the whole, very great, but, from the wonder having ceased, that a boy of thirteen years of age, or thereabouts, could possibly sustain characters, with propriety and effect, that have so frequently baffled the attempts of maturer age'. He must now be judged as an established first-rate actor, 'who may be seen with an abundance of pleasure; though not, perhaps, with that astonishment his first appearance very naturally created'.

These being preliminary performances, the critic was not yet able to assess the new company, though he implies the need for further strength, and complains that the musical department appears to be in a miserable condition. Mrs. Young, however, wife of the new manager, has agreeably surprised him. He had not expected Mrs. Bellamy's place to be adequately filled, but Mrs. Young came closer to doing so than he had thought possible. She lacked 'that exquisite feeling, wherewith Mrs. Bellamy so powerfully reaches the hearts of her audience', but with more experience and 'a little more of her husband's tuition' she would do well.

The company assembled by Ward and Young was very different from that of the previous season. The Bellamys, Gordon,[72] Huddart, Penson, Richardson and Davies had gone. In the newcomers 'A Constant Reader' can find little to praise. He gives an amusing account of Andrews's mannerisms: 'seldom does he speak but he holds his right hand clenched, a little below his breast and, generally, his left arm crooked, or behind him, as if ready, as soon as he may have finished his speech, to knock down the person who stands before him'. Ditcher is in the same class, Romer has ability in low comedy, Spencer, one gathers, is not good, but better than anyone coming from the Stockport theatre had any right to be; and Smith, from Liverpool, 'a handsome young fellow, and a good singer, though less, if possible, of an actor, than Mr. Bellamy; he has a sweet mellow voice' but he lacked Bellamy's knowledge of music and his scientific method of singing.

There was also Hamerton, returned after several years, and much improved. The critic thought he resembled Johnstone on the stage, as he performed Irish characters, and in general compensated for the departure of Richardson. Mrs. Young continued to grow in favour; 'her Amelrosa is certainly a treat I did not expect to have found out of London'. As singing lady, Miss Stephens was pleasing: 'yet her very singular appearance renders her not so agreeable a performer as might be wished'.

Young, in his capacity as manager, is given the credit for introducing much novelty. As an actor, take him all in all, he was of the first rate 'yet I decidedly give the preference to his tragedy'. His Hamlet gave great satisfaction, but although in some genteel comedy parts he never failed to please, in others he was less successful.

The regular season had opened on December 30, 1805, with *Jane Shore* in which Mrs. Young played Jane, her hushusband Hastings, and the evergreen Mrs. Ward, Alicia. As afterpiece *Rosina,* which over the years was bearing out Küttner's praise, was given, with Miss Stephens and Smith in the principal parts. These two, it may be mentioned in passing, were married at Liverpool in the following June.

Among the novelties already referred to, there were Colman's *Who Wants a Guinea, The Delinquents* by Reynolds, Mrs. Inchbald's *To Marry or Not to Marry,* and an odd concoction by Andrew Cherry called *The Travellers; or Music's Fascination* described as 'an Operatic drama'. When the benefits started Miss Ward chose *The Road to Ruin,* which gave Young his first opportunity of playing Dornton. This was followed by a revival of Garrick's *Jubilee Pageant.* For Young's benefit *The Rivals* was given, with Young as Falkland and his wife Julia.

The season had a tragic end. On July 11, less than a month after the theatre had finished its programme with a visit from John Emery, Mrs. Young died of fever after giving birth to her first child. The *Mercury* of July 15, after recording the fact, continued: 'the loss of this most excellent lady will be deeply deplored, not only by her relatives and friends but by every admirer of personal virtue and theatrical merit. In her private character she was truly amiable, affable and sincere; and in her public, excellence itself. In short, the British stage may justly be said to have lost one of its brightest ornaments'. She was not yet twenty-two at the time of her death.

Young's biography was written by his son,[73] and in it he tells of the premonition his mother had of her coming death, and how, when she and her husband were walking in what was then the rural district of Prestwich, she expressed a desire to be buried in the churchyard there. Her wish was granted and some lines composed by Joseph Aston were placed on the tombstone. In the biography, J. C. Young writes of the happiness of their short period in Manchester, and of their notice by the county families and leading manu-

facturers. Oddly, he does not seem aware that his father
was joint-manager, for he writes 'although they received
many lucrative offers from other towns, they preferred to
accept one for a twelvemonth at Manchester', and goes on to
speak of the favourable terms offered them. The biographer
makes another slip, for he gives the date of his mother's
death as July 17.

During the same season, active steps had begun towards
the erection of a new theatre. On January 14, 1806, the
Mercury contained a notice to builders, inviting tenders on
the plan which could be inspected at the Concert Tavern, the
building to be completed, not later than September 29, 1807.
On April 1 the same paper noted that the new building, in
Fountain Street, was in process of erection by Mr. Bellhouse.
Three months later the *Monthly Mirror* announced that Mr.
Macready had obtained a lease of the new Theatre Royal.
Ward and Young, in conjunction with the Liverpool managers, had offered £1,300 per annum, and Raymond, whom
we have noted as a member of the Manchester company but
now of Drury Lane, £1,200; but Macready was willing to
pay £1,600 and to promise a free annual benefit for any
public charity. It was a piece of optimism he was to regret
all too soon.

There was still another season to go at the old theatre.
Before it opened Young had signed a contract with Colman
which was to start him on a distinguished London career,
but this was not to take effect until the close of his Manchester season. The company included old favourites in
Bengough, Swendall, Penson, Turpin, Hamerton and Smith;
among the ladies Mrs. and Miss Ward, Mrs. Smith (lately
Miss Stephens) Mrs. Hatton and Mrs. Powell were well
known in the theatre. There were a few newcomers, and the
Mercury, in an unwonted burst of enthusiasm, said 'the company has never been surpassed and very seldom equalled, in

the town', which has the quality of an effusive obituary notice rather than an objective comment.

Novelties again took a large share in the programmes. Dimond's *Adrian and Orilla, Arbitration* by Reynolds, the Drury Lane melodrama *Takeli,* Tobin's last play, *The Curfew*; these were some plays which received a first hearing locally. *Hamlet* 'being the last time of its being performed by the present company', was given on February 13 with Young in the title part, Mrs. Ward as the Queen and Miss Norton, a newcomer, as Ophelia.

The last round of benefits began. Miss Ward chose *Lovers Vows* in which she played Amelia to Young's Frederick. On May 8 Young appeared as Benedick for his benefit. There was then a visit from Mr. and Mrs. Stephen Kemble. Kemble, said to be the only Falstaff to play the part without stuffing (though in more recent days Oscar Asche was to do so) appeared in that part, with Young as Hotspur.

All was set for the grand finale. The managers had prepared the right curtain by engaging Cooke for six nights beginning on June 15. The day arrived, but not Cooke. Knowing that gentleman, the managers evidently still did not give up hope, for it was not until June 23 that the following notice appeared:

> Theatre Royal, Manchester. The Managers, in the most respectful manner, acquaint the public that they are under the disagreeable necessity, from Mr. Cooke's not coming to fulfil his engagement, to close the Theatre Royal before the expiration of their term, and not to admit any further disappointment to the town. To the ladies and gentlemen of Manchester, and the inhabitants in general, Messrs. Ward and Young beg leave to return thanks for their favours conferred, with every assurance of retaining the obligation in their minds with the liveliest gratitude.

Clearly, their thoughts about Cooke were less kindly. His action was the more reprehensible in that an advance payment had been made to him. They sued him for this amount and obtained judgment. Cooke was in his customary state of financial crisis, and being unable to pay, found himself from August to December lodged in Appleby Gaol. One cannot help a passing regret that the annals of Manchester's first Theatre Royal should end on this note. No actor had been more popular in the town and none had given of himself there more splendidly. Nor, one may suspect, had any actor put more money into the pockets of the managers.

1. The Bill is reprinted in J. P. Earwaker, *Local Gleanings*, 1875, vol. iii, p. 311. For a report of the debate see *Parliamentary Register*, vol. ii, p. 122 *et seq.*
2. Among the subscribers were Dr. Thomas Percival, a notable writer on medical subjects (see *D.N.B.*) and William Stevenson, who gives his name to Stevenson Square.
3. *Manchester Guardian*, Apr. 20, 1869, stated that when the building was being demolished in that year the spring which gave its name to Spring Gardens was discovered underneath the stage, still active.
4. On the history of Manchester streets generally see T. Swindells, *Manchester Streets and Manchester Men*, five series, 1906–8. Spring Gardens is in series I, pp. 217-28; Market Street in series II, pp. 201-98.
5. The first *Manchester and Salford Dictionary*, 1772, was published by Mrs. Elizabeth Raffald. It was reissued in 1773 and 1781.
6. Joseph Harrop started the *Manchester Mercury* in 1752. It was published weekly on Tuesday. J. E. Taylor (founder of the *Manchester Guardian*) bought it in 1825 and it ceased publication in 1830. See W. E. A. Axon, *The Annals of Manchester*, 1886.
7. Tate Wilkinson, *The Wandering Patentee*, 1795, vol. i, pp. 36 and 233 *et seq.* See also R. J. Broadbent, *Annals of the Liverpool Stage*, 1908, *passim.*
8. John Bernard, *Retrospections of the Stage*, 1830, vol. i, p. 3.
9. Unless otherwise stated, references to performances and other theatrical details throughout are from the files of the *Manchester Mercury* (available on microfilm and complete for the period) and/or the collection of playbills, in the Central Reference Library, Manchester.
10. On the benefit system generally see R. J. Broadbent, *Stage Whispers*, 1901, and V. C. Clinton-Baddeley, *All Right on the Night*, 1954, p. 124–8, 148 *et seq.*
11. Addl. MSS. 40, 166/106. I am indebted to Miss Sybil Rosenfeld for drawing my attention to this document and making a transcript.
12. This date may be assumed from the list of deductions from salaries. Only in 1777-8 were all those named in the document members of the company at the same time.
13. R. J. Broadbent, *Annals of the Manchester Stage*, 1735–1844, unpublished, typescript in Manchester Central Reference Library, bound in 3 vols. Unless otherwise stated, all subsequent references to Broadbent will be to this work.
14. Wilkinson, *Wandering Patentee*, vol. pp. 253-4.
15. Daniel Lysons and subsequent editors, *Annals of the Three Choirs*, 1895, p. 44 and footnote, which give some biographical details.

16. Wilkinson, *Wandering Patentee*, vol. i, pp. 259 *et seq.*

17. P. J. de Loutherbourg. Manchester found several eccentric ways of spelling his name.

18. See Cecil Price, "Joseph Austin and his Associates 1766-89", Theatre Notebook, 1950, vol. iv, p. 89. For the period 1758–61 his appearances at Drury Lane are recorded in D. MacMillan, *Drury Lane Calendar*, 1938. He is mentioned in Charles Churchill, *The Rosciad*, 1761 ('Austin would always rustle in french silks.') He died Mar. 31, 1821. Oxberry's *Dramatic Biography*, 1825, gives his age as 81 and this is followed by *Who's Who in the Theatre*, but the *Observer*, Apr. 9, 1821, stated it to be 86.

19. *The Theatric Tourist,* 1805, p. 44

20. There does not seem to be any documentary evidence for these legends. Whitlock, in each of the towns visited, advertised as a dentist.

21. See Cecil Price, "An 18th Century Theatrical Agreement", *Theatre Notebook*, 1948, vol. ii, p. 31, which discusses a form of actor's agreement used by this company.

22. *Elmira*, a dramatic poem by Edward Stanley (taken from *The Tales of the Genii*), 1790.

23. For amateur theatricals at Wynnstay see Cecil Price, *The English Theatre in Wales*, 1948.

24. There is an article on John Hodgkinson in *Dictionary of American Biography* where he is stated to be a native of Manchester. Otherwise there is nothing useful on his English career. The playbill for June 23, 1788, at the Theatre Royal, Newcastle, announced his 'first appearance these three years'. His last appearance there was Apr. 29, 1789. When Austin and Whitlock were there in August neither Hodgkinson nor "Mrs. Munden" was with them.

25. Wilkinson, *Wandering Patentee*, vol. ii, p. 67.

26. MacMillan, *Calendar*, pp. 189, 191.

27. Wilkinson, *Wandering Patentee,* vol. iii, p. 87.

28. W. Dunlap, *Memoirs of George Frederick Cooke*, 2nd. edn., vol. i, p. 35.

29. Wilkinson engaged the Marshalls for York Race Week, 1782, and comments on them in *Wandering Patentee*, vol. i, p. 143. Marshall had first appeared at the Haymarket in 1781: *Thespian Dictionary*, 1802. Mrs. Marshall 'died a few days ago at North Shields', *Mercury,* Jan. 4, 1791. Marshall made American debut in 1793 and returned to England in 1801.

30. Axon, *Annals of Manchester*, pp. 109, 111, 112.

31. B. Faujas de Saint Fond, *A Journey through England and Scotland in 1784*, trans. Sir Archibald Geikie, 1907, vol. ii, p. 267.

32. *Thespian Dictionary* states that Banks's father had been Harlequin at Sadler's Wells. The son returned to London and was

engaged at Drury Lane. 'His taste and execution in scene paint-ing renders him useful to theatres.'

33. Dunlap, *Cooke*, vol. i, p. 39.

34. This benefit was on Apr. 25. *Philander and Rose* does not appear to have been published, but the songs 'by Griffith Cheese' were printed in 1785. Cheese died Nov. 10, 1804: Axon, *Annals of Manchester,* p. 134.

35. Wilkinson, *Wandering Patentee*, vol. ii, p. 188.

36. Axon, *Annals*, pp. 111-2.

37. Axon, *ibid*, p. 112, is incorrect in giving date as Sep. 1.

38. The Whitfields were engaged for Garrick's last season at Drury Lane, 1775–6: MacMillan, *Calendar*, p. 204 *et seq*. At that time Mrs. Whitfield's roles seem to have been better than her hus-band's. See also *Thespian Dictionary*.

39. Mrs. Warrall (there given as 'Warrell') is in *Thespian Dictionary*: 'her person, voice and action are agreeable.'

40. Gilliband says 'Mattocks shortly after failed.' *Dramatic Mirror*, 1808, vol. i, p. 221.

41. For some nights in March the afterpieces were contributed by a 'Company of Italians'. On March 28 'Signor, Father of the Family' promised 'a Dance between Eggs blindfold without breaking them.'

42. Miss Eccles is praised by Wilkinson, *Wandering Patentee*, vol. iii, p. 14. He states that she later played at Norwich in her real name of Edmead.

43. Wilkinson has much to say about Wood in *Wandering Patentee*, vol. i, p. 96 *et seq*.

44. Wilkinson says of Mrs. Smith (who came to him from Dublin) 'she acquitted herself well, and promised to be what she after-wards proved, a great favourite.' *Wandering Patentee*, vol. ii, p. 77. On Smith he is silent.

45. This can hardly be correct. An adaptation from Jonson's *The Alchemist* under this name was written by Francis Gentleman and first played in Edinburgh about 1760. It is conceivable that Colman had revised it for Kippling.

46. It was during this visit that Cooke's encounter with Perrins the pugilist occurred as related by Ryley in *The Itinerant*, vol. iii, pp. 74–9.

47. *Thespian Dictionary* states that Bowden was first apprenticed in the cotton trade and then in business on his own account. There does not appear to be any confirmation of this, though he seems to have been accepted as a native of Manchester.

48. Broadbent states 'it has been conjectured that Penn was the name adopted at this time by an actor subsequently well-known as Penson.' This seems most unlikely. When Penson joined Wilkin-son in October of this year, and throughout his career, he was a low comedian. On Dec. 12 of the same year an actor named Penn played Jaques with Thomas Bibby's company (Margaret

Baron-Wilson, *Memoirs of Harriot, Duchess of St. Albans*, 1840, vol. i, p. 87.) This seems more likely to have been the man.

49. Wilkinson, *Wandering Patentee*, vol. i, p. 62.

50. R. W. Procter, *Manchester in Holiday Dress*, 1866, p. 97.

51. Wilkinson says of Mrs. Davis, 'she is young, very pretty, a more than promising actress in Mrs. Jordan's cast of parts, has great life and much merit.' He continues that she was much approved at Birmingham, Margate, and Hull more so than at Manchester. 'She was seduced from a good engagement at Manchester to engage at Covent Garden, in February, 1792': *Wandering Patentee*, vol. i, p. 79. *Mercury*, Nov. 2, 1790, contains a note: 'Mrs. Davis, who performs the principal comic characters at our theatre, is not, as is generally supposed, the "cara sposa" of the gentleman who bears the same name with this our favourite Thalia, but the wife of a celebrated comedian, who performed under the banners of Garrick, Foote, Barry and the heroes of old.'

52. *The Torrington Diary*, ed. C. B. Andrews, 4 vols., 1934–8, vol. ii, p. 206.

53. Of Swendall *Thespian Dictionary* says 'He is correct and energetic, and it is surprising that his abilities did not recommend him to Drury Lane as the best substitute for Mr. Aickin'. Swendall became manager at Brighton. His wife was a sister of Jack Bannister.

54. Thomas Dibdin, *Reminiscences*, 1827, vol. i, p. 110 *et seq.* for all Manchester references here quoted.

55. Wilkinson, *Wandering Patentee*, vol. iv, pp. 55–6.

56. *ibid.* vol. iii, p. 126.

57. *Mercury*, May 28, 1793, announced the marriage 'on Thursday, May 23, at the Collegiate Church, Mr. Merchant, of our Theatre, to Miss Hilliar, of the Bolton Theatre. Among the wedding guests figured Cooke, Ryley and John Moorhead the musician, the bridegroom's theatrical associates for the time being.'

58. According to Swindells, *Manchester Streets*, Series II, p. 189, the circus was built by Ward and Banks at a cost of £1,000. I cannot find any confirmation of this, and Swindells does not supply references, but I have found him consistently accurate. The circus seems generally to have been sublet to visiting companies.

59. One would like to know much more of Mrs. Shepley. Over a long period no oratorio or concert over a wide area seems to have been complete without her, and she often sang alongside artists of international fame. Biographical details, however, are lacking.

60. Handy announced that he paid to eleven members of his company the sum of £56 per week, but that nevertheless his prices were two shillings, one shilling, and sixpence.

61. For the National Anthem in the theatre see Clinton-Baddeley, *All Right on the Night*, p. 89 *et seq.* and Percy Scholes, *God Save the King*, 1954, *passim*.

62. Wilkinson, *Wandering Patentee*, vol. ii, p. 13. Accounts of Cherry are in *D.N.B.*, *Thespian Dictionary*, and *Dramatic Mirror*. His Swansea period as manager is discussed in Cecil Price, *English Theatre in Wales*, 1948, p. 93 *et seq.*

63. *Mirror*, vol. iii, 1797, pp. 118–9,

64. *ibid.* 1798, vol. vi, p. 182.

65. Wilkinson says of Penson, 'He is now a favourite, and greatly esteemed throughout the whole circuit; has much unusual merit; good private behaviour to establish his public worth; and a study his superiors gaze with wonder at.' *Wandering Patentee*, vol. iii, p. 93.

66. *Memoirs of Charles Dibdin, the Younger,* ed. George Speaight, 1956, pp. 36, 37.

67. The wedding was reported in the *Mercury*, May 9, 1802.

68. *Monthly Mirror* published a metrical account of the company from Chester.

69. Of James Watson, Swindells, Series I, p. 69, says, 'He was one of those whose genius and ability are overclouded by a complete want of will-power. Although possessed with a talent for the stage, which enabled him to take a lead in amateur theatricals and brought him in personal contact with many actors, amongst whom was G. F. Cooke, the eminent tragedian; and also some literary talent, as shown in his poems, published under the title of *The Spirit of the Doctor,* his life was a complete failure. Appointed librarian when the Portico was opened in 1806, he soon lost that position in consequence of his drinking habits and neglect of duty'.

70. Philip Worrall was one of the best-known and best-loved men of his time in Manchester. He was a hairdresser, first in Blue Boar Court and later in Market Place, as well as his employment at the theatre. Ryley speaks of him with affection in *The Itinerant* and his benefits, continued as a gesture after financial misfortune had overtaken him, were always well attended. He died on Apr. 4, 1811.

71. Details of these receipts were: Nov. 12, £150 3s.; Nov. 13, £155 9s.; Nov. 14, £156 2s.; Nov. 15, £153 5s.; Nov. 16, £165 5s; Nov. 17, £122 2s.; Nov. 19, £169; Nov. 20 (benefit), £300.

72. Bellamy and Gordon had become joint managers of the theatre at Belfast.

73. J. C. Young, *Memoirs of Charles Mayne Young by his son*, 1871, pp. 21 *et seq.*

INDEX

1. PLAYS

Acis and Galatea, 13, 43, 125
Adopted Child, The, 143
Adrian and Orilla, 174
Agreeable Surprise, The, 136
Alchemist, The, 124, 178
Alexander the Great, 36
All for Love, 85
All in the Wrong, 34, 88
All the World's a Stage, 101
Almira, 120
Anna Bullen (see Virtue Betray'd)
Anne Boleyn, or The Innocent Sacrifice, 7
Arbitration, 174
As You Like It, 31, 63, 83, 119, 126, 148, 158

Battle of Hexham, The, 133
Beaux Stratagem, The, 28, 36, 89, 100, 127, 140
Beggar's Opera, The, 75, 114, 134, 139
Beggar on Horseback, The, 136
Belle's Stratagem, The, 98, 160
Birth and Adventures of Harlequin, The, 93
Blue Beard, 154
Bold Stroke for a Husband, A, 127
Bold Stroke for a Wife, A, 37

Camp, The, 96, 141
Cape St. Vincent, 149
Castle of Andalusia, The, 104
Castle Spectre, The, 151, 155
Cato, 6, 25, 105, 122
Chrononhotonthologos, 102
Cinderella, 166
City Wives' Confederacy, The, 42
Civilian, The, 127
Clandestine Marriage, The, 41, 43, 88, 99
Cleone, 88, 114
Codrus, 66, 94
Comedy of Errors, The, 98, 145
Comus, 28, 139
Conscious Lovers, The, 89
Constant Couple, The, 36
Coriolanus, 88, 140
Countess of Salisbury, The, 90
Critic, The, 97, 127, 148
Cure for a Scold, The, 46, 71
Cure for the Heart Ache, A, 149
Curfew, The, 174
Cymbeline, 63, 96, 102, 121, 154
Cymon, 86
Cyrus, 89

Death of Capt. Cook, The, 134
Death of General Wolfe, The, 134
Delinquents, The, 172
Deserter, The, 72
Deuce is in Him, The, 37, 71
Devil to Pay, The, 93
Discovery, The, 71
Distrest Mother, The, 89
Double Gallant, The, 89
Douglas, 87, 105, 120, 143, 153, 167
Dramatist, The, 133
Duenna, The, 96
Duke of Braganza, The, 140
Duplicity, 101

Earl of Warwick, The, 62, 122, 147
Edward and Eleanora, 154
Edward the Black Prince, 94
Elmira, 98, 101, 177
Every One has his Fault, 146
Execution of Harlequin, The (see The Royal Hunters)

Fair Em, or The Miller's Daughter of Manchester, 4
Fair Penitent, The, 6, 46, 88, 120
False Delicacy, 87
Farmer, The, 134
Female Officer, The (Brooke), 36
Female Officer, The (Kemble), 94
First Love, 143
Follies of a Day, 115
Force of Love, The (see Theodosius)
Foundling, The, 102
Funeral, The, 42

Gamester, The, 160
Gentle Shepherd, The, 28
George Barnwell (see The London Merchant)
Gil Blas, 139
Grecian Daughter, The, 55, 88, 94, 105

Hamlet, 48, 63, 88, 95, 103, 105, 109-10, 114, 115, 119, 121, 124, 125, 127, 132, 134, 137, 142, 145, 151, 153, 160, 163, 167, 171, 174
Harlequin Dr. Faustus, 85, 93, 120
Harlequin Foundling, 118
Harlequin Mungo, 126
Harlequin's Invasion, 115
Heir at Law, The, 150
Heiress, The, 119
Henry II, 72, 94
Henry IV, 39, 63, 85, 93, 97, 105, 174

2. PERSONS AND SUBJECTS